More praise for *The Complexity Advantage*

"Kelly and Allison use the vocabulary of the sciences of complexity and apply it to real-world problems of managing software and development, offering lessons of emergence, co-evolution, and increasing returns to help managers navigate the transition from hierarchical structures to market structures."
Henry A. Lichstein
Vice President, Breakout Strategies, Advanced Development Group, Citibank Trustee of The Santa Fe Institute

"Translates the lessons of this new science of complexity to real-world situations and options facing business leaders."
David R. Johnson
Advisor to the Internet Policy Project, The Aspen Institute

"Provides valuable guidance for leaders who will propel corporations into the next level of management."
Stephen Cross
Director, Software Engineering Institute

"Provides practical tools for anyone in the business community looking for competive advantage."
Doug Johnson
General Manager, Hewlett-Packard Laser Jet Supplies

"This is a book for business, and an excellent guide to intelligent implementation."
John Philpin
Internet Consultant

Other BusinessWeek Books

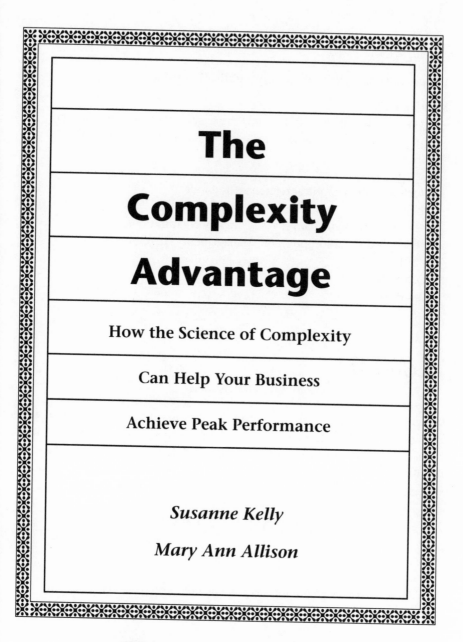

The

Complexity

Advantage

How the Science of Complexity

Can Help Your Business

Achieve Peak Performance

Susanne Kelly

Mary Ann Allison

 **BusinessWeek Books**

McGraw-Hill

New York   San Francisco   Washington, D.C.   Auckland   Bogotá
Caracas   Lisbon   London   Madrid   Mexico City   Milan
Montreal   New Delhi   San Juan   Singapore
Sydney   Tokyo   Toronto

Library of Congress Cataloging-in-Publication Data

Kelly, Susanne.
   The complexity advantage : how the science of complexity can help
your business achieve peak-performance / Susanne Kelly, Mary Ann
Allison.
      p. cm.
   Includes bibliographical references and index.
   ISBN 0-07-001400-0
   1. Organizational change. 2. Complex organizations.
   3. Complexity (Philosophy) 4. Management. I. Allison, Mary Ann.
  II. Title.
  HD58.8.K458   1998
  658—dc21   98-47604
                                                  CIP

McGraw-Hill

A Division of The **McGraw·Hill** Companies

1 2 3 4 5 6 7 8 9 0 DOC/DOC 9 0 3 2 1 0 9 8

ISBN 0-07-001400-0

*The editing supervisor was Tom Laughman, and the production supervisor was
Pamela A. Pelton. It was set in Stone Serif by North Market Street Graphics.*

Printed and bound by R. R. Donnelley & Sons Company.

McGraw-Hill books are available at special quantity discounts to use as premi-
ums and sales promotions, or for use in corporate training sessions. For more
information, please write to the Director of Special Sales, McGraw-Hill, 11 West
19th Street, New York, NY 10011. Or contact your local bookstore.

To Megan and Tara,
who fill my heart with love and pride.

To Eric, who taught me
win/win before it was well known.

Contents

Section Two: So What if Businesses Are Self-Organizing Systems?

Preface

A Guide to This Book

This book is devoted to new roles, methods, and paradigms arising from new thinking in scientific disciplines. From our own experience, the experiences of those we have worked with, and the results of primary research, we have striking evidence that by understanding these concepts we can change the way we live and work. When properly structured in an evolutionary enterprise fitness model, key concepts from science can be used to enable businesses to sustain leadership positions over long periods of time even in the face of rapid change.

We have assembled ideas from our business experience and the study of traditional sciences as well as Chaos and Complexity Theory, Systems Theory, and new theories of biology and evolution. Together they give rise to our own theories of emergent social systems. In the sciences, as in any human endeavor, there are various—sometimes conflicting—schools of thought. Although several practicing scientists have validated our interpretation of scientific theory, we have made no attempt to present a comprehensive picture of the state of any particular line of research. Instead, in Section 1, "The Complexity Advantage," we have presented only the most relevant concepts—chosen for their ability to generate business success.

In Section 2, "So What if Businesses Are Self-Organizing Systems?," at the heart of this book, we describe in our practical prescriptions for businesses:

- The Four Simple Rules *that enable businesses to identify, undo, and redo the patterns of dysfunctional behavior, which make it impossible for them to move quickly (Chapters 5 and 6)*

- The Fourteen Steps for Success, *which provide clear direction enabling businesses to use complexity science to generate competitive advantages (Chapter 7)*

- The Complexity Advantage Evolutionary Fitness Model, *which describes a method of increasing business capabilities built on the concepts taken from the latest understanding of self-organization and evolution (Chapters 8 and 9)*

We know these rules, steps, and models work because we have tried it both ways. In real-world situations ranging from multinational corporations to Internet start-ups, we have worked with and without the benefit of these ideas.

In Section 3, "Working in a Living System," we follow these prescriptions with descriptions of how business people in various roles—as agents, leaders, catalysts, and eco-technicians—apply The Complexity Advantage paradigm on the job.

Section 4, "Experiencing The Advantage," includes a chapter in which business leaders from Citibank talk directly about their experiences with conscious evolution. The last chapter has two parts. In the first part we demonstrate how to use the key complexity science concepts to analyze business dynamics by applying them to Citibank's recent history. We conclude by providing a summary of the basics of *The Complexity Advantage,* a quick reference guide for those who want to get started right away.

The final test will be whether you find these principles work for you. Just as we learned from many others in the course of developing this model, we hope that many of you will help to develop this line of thinking even further. We are eager to have that dialog with you and to continue our own learning.

Heartfelt Thanks to All Those Who Helped as We Wrote *The Complexity Advantage*

No book of this scope is ever written without the help of many people, both those living and those who lived long before. Going back at least to Newton and Darwin, we are grateful to those whose ideas, research, and experiences contributed to our thinking and models. Current business leaders, scientists, and other authors provided useful critiques and shared their experiences generously. At a time when editors do more sales work and less editing, Mary Glenn, our editor at McGraw-Hill, patiently and intelligently walked us through the difficult process of cutting the original manuscript, which was far too dense and long. Our families and friends provided essential and immediate support in the way that only those who love you can . . . by being there, by reading innumerable drafts and listening sympathetically, by making dinner and eating alone for the 20th day in a row, by sharing last holiday season with "The Grinch Who Stole Christmas," and, most importantly, by believing in us.

Although we can't mention everyone, there are some who stand out in our hearts and minds. As you know well what you did, we will content ourselves in most cases with listing your names.

Susanne especially thanks parents Betty and Gerry Newton for her nature and early nurture, and she thanks mentor, Colin Crook, for perturbing so many new possibilities. Daughters, Megan and Tara, are much appreciated for their support, inspiration, and understanding. In addition, thanks go to Mary Ann and Eric Allison, Mary Beth Chrisis, Marshall Clemens and Karin DelSignore (for graphics), Jodie Hansen, Liz Kaufman, Steve Lafredo, Michael Lissack, Eve Mitleton-Kelly, Mark Paulk, Bill Peterson, Dennis Shiel, Michael Veale, Yaneer Bar Yam, and Lee Zimskind. Plus, special thanks to so many unnamed friends from Citibank, SEI, and the Complex-M list who broadened my experience and triggered my thinking.

Mary Ann wants to thank: Alex Barakov (and the whole Sunday morning Karate family), Barbara Blair, David and Mary Burnet, Michael and Vickie Burnet, Marshall Clemens, Karen Erickson, Larry Golde, Russ James, Tom Hoover, Susanne Kelly, Grace Mangum, Michael Lissack, Dante Mancini, John Philpin, John and Sheila Nedrow, Chris Nystrom, Richard Ryan, Dennis Sheil, Anthony Spina, Dominic Spina (Chapter 13 is for you), Geoff Squire, Karen Sunde ("impressed but not surprised" carried me many days), Jo, John, and Amy Jo Tiedeman, Tyler Volk, Bill Washburn, and Ann Wiseman. First, last, and always, my thanks and love to Eric.

Introduction

Managing in a Complex World
By Colin Crook, Chief Technology Officer, Citicorp, Retired

By now it is apparent that managers of enterprises and their employees have been, overall, victims of many so-called management fads. These fads have appeared relentlessly over the years, each succeeding wave causing increased questioning of the whole business process. Surely some more fundamental and enduring theory and insight regarding the business enterprise is possible.

The emergence of complex self-organizing systems theory and the whole edifice of complexity science has the potential for providing the conceptual basis for such a fundamental business theory. It can help to explain how enterprises, their employees, customers, and the environment behave.

This prospect for theoretical progress is becoming more widely recognized. A simple measure is the appearance of an increasingly large number of books that mention complexity theory and so forth in their titles. A review of these books and publications reveals a mixed bag. Clearly these are still early days. An extremely important missing ingredient is the total lack of both operational data and practical steps for moving various theories into practice.

We often see somewhat mystical interpretations of many scientific theories appearing as management science. Other books purport to be based upon operating data from the real world of business and economics. One can be forgiven a certain skepticism concerning the validity of such claims. Nonetheless, the overall effect of these books and publications is to suggest that we do have the prospect of real progress in developing an overall theory regarding how businesses and their markets behave. Complex adaptive systems theory looks very promising. But it is still in its infancy.

Certain work undertaken at Citicorp during the past several years in areas relating to process, software, architecture, organizational behavior, and the use of complexity theory has provided some valuable insight. Major initiatives, such as the Software Engineering Institute's Capability Maturity Model (CMM), undertaken over a period of six years and involving 5000 software professionals, have provided extensive operational data. The leading-edge use of complexity theory within Citicorp, often with excellent operational results, has provided increasing familiarity with these difficult concepts. In all, a rich soup of experimental and theoretical activity has generated much-needed data. However, important insights derived from this rich soup were not always apparent to line management, preoccupied with their "normal" tasks.

Susanne Kelly worked extremely hard and with great creativity to bring about progress and acceptance of the SEI's CMM in Citicorp. During this period, she invented and debugged breakthrough methods for teaching and communicating the essence of the CMM. She took advantage of the experimental and theoretical "complexity" activity going on around her to synthesize new and fundamentally different ways of bringing about organizational change and behavior. She shared her findings with longtime friend and colleague Mary Ann Allison.

At the same time, Mary Ann moved from Citicorp to cofound an Internet start-up venture and The Allison Group, LLC, a management consulting company, specializing in strategic planning, organizational development, and the stimulated growth of virtual business communities. She began integrating the complexity thinking with her work and postgraduate research into the nature of community, proving these complexity concepts ever more powerful.

Inspired, they joined forces to expand upon and record the original Citicorp work. This book reflects their insight, experience, and creativity. It represents an important body of practical knowledge aligned to the new world of complexity science and leaves the old world of transitory management fads behind.

The Complexity Advantage

Chapter One

The Complexity Advantage

This book will enable businesses to use complexity science to thrive in the complex global markets emerging from the information revolution—no matter how often or how drastically these markets change. The complexity advantage is not just critical to business executives and leaders, but to all contributors in the business community. Business communities comprising participants who understand and apply complexity-based paradigms will have enthusiastic employee contribution, better information, dramatic increases in both productivity and creativity, lower costs, and the ability to respond rapidly to change in direction.

The focused beam of light generated by a laser is hundreds of times more powerful than an ordinary light beam from the 100-watt bulb in a desk lamp. Ordinary, *incoherent* light consists of waves of many frequencies, in all phases, and moving in all directions. Light waves in the laser beam are coherent, organized at the same frequency and phase, and traveling in the same direction. This gives a laser the power to cut through even very dense materials that are normally difficult to penetrate with precision.

The power and precision of a laser comes from the organization of its individual light waves. Although the mechanisms that provide energy and a suitable environment for laser beam generation are manufactured, the remarkable thing about a laser is that the light waves *organize themselves.*

A laser beam is a complex self-organizing system. So are all living things. All social systems, which are societies of living things, are complex self-organizing systems as well.

The Main Point: Self-Organization

Your business comprises self-organizing systems whether you know it or like it. You can cut costs and improve profits dramatically by learning to work with these systems rather than against them. So, what is self-organization and how does it work?

Self-organization is a fundamental principle of the universe in which we live and work. Open, self-organizing systems use energy, material, and feedback (information) from their internal and external environments to organize themselves. Because energy is used up—or dissipated—in the course of the organization, self-organizing systems are also called *dissipative systems*. This process is not directed or controlled by a conscious entity, but rather emerges through the interrelationships of the system's parts. Self-organization takes place only under certain conditions in a state called *bounded instability*. This state is often described by complexity theorists as being *at the edge of chaos*.

Every self-organizing system is unique. Each emerges from a specific history and interacts with an environment that—while it may seem similar to—is never exactly the same as that for another system. A self-organizing system produces results that are different and more powerful than those that could be produced by the parts of that system working independently.

In this book, we build on complexity science to explain and apply the principles of self-organization to business and organizational behavior. We discuss the enterprise environment and energy that leaders must provide to generate the power and precision of laser-sharp business performance. This performance is attained through the coherence and collaboration of all of the people contributing to that business community.

Complexity Science

Complexity science is the name commonly used to describe a set of interdisciplinary studies that share the idea that all things tend to self-organize into systems. Physics, biology, chemistry, chaos theory, cybernetics, synergetics, and nonlinear dynamics are among the many fields that are a part of the complexity tradition.

Surprisingly, the enormous diversity of systemic patterns described by complexity science does not come from some elaborate scientific principles or labyrinthine processes. Instead, the patterns come from a simple set of rules applied over and over again to the latest results in a sequential process called *recursion.* This is why even very small differences at the start of the process can produce very large accumulated differences in later performance.

Complexity advantage companies understand the nature of open systems and bounded instability (more about this later). In doing so, they can build on capabilities that have emerged through billions of years of experience called *evolution* (or, more precisely, co-evolution, as many open systems evolve interactively).

Complexity advantage companies address today's transition in business—plagued by rapid change and increasing uncertainty. For approximately a century, our manufacturing model was comparatively stable. Rules for productivity, market dominance, and corporate or personal success were well understood. The Information Age has turned previous "knowns" upside-down. Today, no one can predict what or how rapidly new technologies and applications will be developed; no one can determine the precise ways in which the supply chain will be affected or customers will respond; and no one knows exactly how the global financial markets will perform. The best business plan is only a best guess. Table 1.1 summarizes the old and new business paradigms. Today, most businesses are caught somewhere in between.

By the way, if you are part of a start-up or a small-to-medium-sized business, don't be fooled by the adjective "global." Today, satellite communications, the Internet, and air transport move information, materials, products, and people rapidly from place to place. All of us are now connected through a global market comprising mail-order customers and suppliers, supply chain partnerships, and international franchise competition. Even our local pizza parlor has installed a fax machine and is

TABLE 1.1
**Manufacturing Age Business Transitioning
to Information Age Business**

	Manufacturing Age Business	Information Age Business
Game	Bulk-material manufacturing	Design and use of technology
Goal	Commodity products	Knowledge-based products
Domain	Regional	Global
Future	Predictability, deterministic	Uncertainty, probability, possibility
Change	Periodic nuance, steady rate, digestible	Way of life: accelerating, overwhelming
Rules	Linear cause and effect	Nonlinear complex interaction
Game Plan	Five-year strategic plans	Three-year probability scenarios
Leader	Manages strategic plan to end state	Envisions and coaches on direction
Ownership	Centralized decision-making and responsibility	Distributed decision-making and responsibility
Challenge	Demand versus capacity to deliver	Demand versus capacity for change
Resources	Material and financial capital	Human, social, or intellectual capital
Risk	Moving too quickly—out of control	Moving too slowly—out of the running
Approach	Quality, low cost of production	Be first—best if possible, high-cost R&D
	Branding, emergent price standards	Market lock-on, high margins
	Diminishing returns	Increasing returns
Role of the Team	Optimization of quality and productivity	Quality = productivity = adaptability
	Application of raw energy	Application of ideas
	Repetitive day-to-day operations	Quest for innovation
	Processing of resources	Processing of information
Process Perspective	Parts interact in sequence of steps	Whole emerges from interacting parts
	End-to-end efficiency key, standardization the answer	Micro- to macrointegrity key, feedback the answer

designing a Web site. They must compete not only with the deli down the street, but also with global fast-food chains such as McDonald's, Burger King, and Pizza Hut. Without the complexity advantage, they risk the fate of dinosaurs.

Complexity advantage companies develop agents with the ability to self-organize rapidly and to redirect efforts of the whole company or selected parts. Their agents use complexity science to transform rapidly with the environment, searching for new possibilities and redirecting quickly from within. This ability to change generates the capacity to respond naturally and powerfully to avalanches of change—occurring either in the form of opportunities or potential disasters.

Businesses that don't use *The Complexity Advantage* will be at the mercy of an increasing number of sudden and unexpected shifts in the marketplace, called *avalanches*. As uncertainty grows exponentially with today's high rate of technological change and the fallout from it, so does the resultant pressure of global markets. Many leaders try to respond to this uncertainty with yesterday's mind-set and linear cause-and-effect techniques. Often, these responses simply intensify vicious internal cycles of ineffective behavior. Despite well-conceived strategies and well-intended actions, command-and-control management drives inevitable self-organization underground. Covert actions and hidden processes are the genesis of management surprises that impact or delay product development and delivery.

The Information Age: Competing in a Complex World

The increased pressure from rapid change and global competition continually pushes business leaders *to do something*. And, so, we do more of what has worked for us in the past or try the new flavor-of-the-month management fad (such as total quality management [TQM], reengineering, benchmarking, knowledge management). Frequently, these actions disrupt the networks of experienced staff who have the knowledge, experience, and connections to make the business successful. Then, instead of increasing effectiveness, leadership actions cause everyone to reconnect and reinvent the wheel or go underground. Things slow down and leaders get impatient again, feeling the need *to do something more* (see Figure 1.1). The question is "What will be more effective?"

The bottom line is that old-fashioned bureaucracies—commanded and controlled by a few leaders—cannot respond to today's rate of change with the speed and precision of numerous coherent, intelligent, and self-disciplined agents who self-organize with integrity and overtly coordinate their co-evolution.

Maximizing Your Return from The Complexity Advantage

To reap the full benefit of the complexity advantage, businesspeople should develop the ability to use the information emerging from complexity sciences in three ways:

1. First, as a mind-set and way of thinking about their businesses and the fitness landscape in which they compete

2. Second, in actually implementing the complexity advantage steps and models in their businesses

FIGURE 1.1
**Dysfunctional Feedback Loop. Rapid Change
and Competitive Pressure.**

3. Third, as a way of examining current and past business performance to understand why certain strategies and models work, while others do not

In this first section of *The Complexity Advantage,* we discuss a set of basic complexity ideas—the understanding of which is essential for a new and powerful approach to business. In addition to the main point of self-organization, there are six concepts that form the basis of the complexity advantage. We discuss these concepts in Chapter 2. Then, in Chapter 3, our discussion of co-evolution and competitive fitness landscapes provides a way to examine your business using a complexity perspective.

With this as a background, we focus on specific tools for improved business leadership and participation—in the form of practical steps, models, and newly defined roles that are critical to success. With these tools, leaders working within the business community can use the complexity advantage's unique and practical steps for success to generate the three types of capital critical to business success in a global marketplace: human, social, and intellectual. These steps, arranged in a complexity advantage evolutionary fitness model, have been tested in a wide range of business settings, from huge multinational corporations to small-but-powerful Internet start-ups. At the end of the book, we show you how we use complexity advantage tools to examine individual and corporate performance.

Chapter Two

Key Complexity Advantage Concepts

T he poet Wallace Stevens once wrote in a letter that "Everything is complicated; if that were not so, life and poetry and everything else would be a bore."[1] In fact, if everything weren't complicated, there would be no life or poetry or business and, as for everything else— because we wouldn't be around—we wouldn't know anything about it.

In this chapter we present six concepts that—although not making complexity simple—are easy to understand and apply. In addition, we begin a discussion of the nature of a business team assembled using these techniques. In Section 4, "Working in a Living System," we return to the business team with a chapter devoted to each of the major roles.

The Complexity Advantage Concepts

The following six concepts are essential to an understanding of how to use complexity science to generate business success.

Concept 1: Nonlinear Dynamics

Although the precise definition of nonlinear dynamics is complicated and best expressed mathematically, the concepts underlying nonlinear dynamics are both comprehensible and critical to any business leader. Linear dynamics are those in which the effects are proportional to the causes. Contrast this with the nonlinear system—where very small differences at the start may lead to vastly different results. This sensitivity to the initial conditions is called the *butterfly effect,* because an early paper used, as an example of this effect, the changes in Texas weather patterns, which might have been the result of a butterfly flapping its wings in Brazil. Astute leaders give the butterfly effect serious attention—particularly at turning points for their businesses, such as launching a new product, starting a new division, or funding a new line of research.

Before the development of computers, scientists recognized that many systems were nonlinear, but the nonlinear equations that defined them simply took too long to solve. Therefore, linear equations have often been substituted to approximate nonlinear systems. As is frequently the case when we extrapolate, we lose the nuances and caveats associated with the actual experience we have in our nonlinear world. Binders of linear project, budget, and business models that portray a highly simplified and inaccurate cause-and-effect picture of organizational interaction are created then ignored, because they bear little resemblance to the dynamics of our unfolding reality. Nonlinear mathematics helps us to model our past experience more realistically for use in forecasting probable future patterns.

Concept 2: Open and Closed Systems

An open system is one in which the boundaries permit interaction with their environment. A good example is a cell within the human body. The cell membrane quite clearly defines the boundaries of the cell, but it also enables nutrients and information (electrical impulses from the nervous system) to enter and waste and information (electrical impulses to the nervous system) to exit. As open systems at a microlevel (cells) are enveloped in a more macro system (human body), they are referred to as *nested open systems* (see Figure 2.1). A

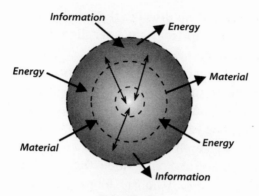

FIGURE 2.1
Nested Open Systems.

closed system neither imports nor exports energy, information, or material.

Many business systems seem only partially open. We all know, for example, of businesses, teams, leaders, and agents who shut out certain kinds of information. Most often they are open only to information that matches the ways in which they already see the world. The more diversity imbedded in organizational components, the less likely this shutting out of information is to happen. It is natural and clearly important to provide some check on the overwhelming amounts of information available. But to compete effectively, it is also critical for businesses to see the changing nature of their customers, competition, and the economic markets in ways that enable them to produce goods and services of genuine value. Those businesses that use tools from *The Complexity Advantage,* such as fitness landscapes (discussed in Chapter 3), will have the benefit of the latest scientific concepts and models to assist them in this task.

Concept 3: Feedback Loops

Business leaders and employees can build on an understanding of feedback loops to eliminate powerful vicious cycles that sabotage personal well-being and organizational success. Vicious cycles sap a company's strength. Once vicious cycles are removed, new feedback loops can be used to develop more positive organizational patterns called *hypercycles*.

Leaders and employees who discover the secret of hypercycles will naturally align their work efforts—as the laser aligns light waves—to deliver razor-sharp performances.

Feedback is the action of *feeding* or reporting *back* to the originator of an action the results of that action. When you introduce a new product, customer response is feedback.

A feedback loop (see Figure 2.2) is simply a series of actions, each of which builds on the results of prior action and *loops* back in a circle to affect the original state. The final action either reinforces or changes the direction of the status quo. Feedback loops can—but do not necessarily—greatly magnify the results of the original event.

There are two types of feedback loops: amplifying and balancing. In an amplifying feedback loop, the direction of the first event is extended by the last event. A series of purchases, which make the stock market go up, which causes more investors to buy, which causes the market to go up again, and so on . . . is an *amplifying feedback loop*. Exactly the opposite is true in a balancing feedback loop: The direction of the first event is reversed or changed by the final action.

The ability to identify and influence feedback loops is a potent business skill. For example, although innovation is an important part of business success, an amplifying feedback loop might exaggerate the amount of innovation to the point at which nothing is ever produced and brought to market. In this situation, an effective complexity advantage leader could identify the amplification and trigger some balancing events. Feedback loops—whether functional or dysfunctional—are a key part of the self-organization that emerges in all businesses.

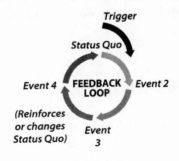

FIGURE 2.2
Open System.

Combining Complexity Concepts 2 and 3:
Closed Behavioral Loops in Open Systems

Feedback loops can be used to describe much of individual and group behavior. Often, powerful feedback loops lull us into ignoring information (see Figure 2.3). Consider the example of young team leaders who do well at guiding their first projects. The most likely result is that they will be pleased by their successes and try leading again. This second time provides more experience, and they get even more comfortable with their successful leadership styles . . . which engenders more success . . . which encourages additional experience . . . and so on. Until, perhaps, they get so ingrained in their approaches they ignore the signals (information) that would indicate their context is changing and they need to change their styles as well. Sometimes small surprises and failures are enough to break a behavioral loop from within; sometimes behavioral loops are shattered from the outside.

Concept 4: Fractal Structures

Fractal structures are those in which the nested parts of a system are shaped into the same pattern as the whole. This is called *self-similarity.* You can see this similarity by comparing an oak leaf with an oak tree. The stem of the leaf is similar to the trunk of the tree, and the veins in the leaf have a pattern that is comparable to the branching from the

FIGURE 2.3
Closed Behavioral Loop in an Open Human System.

trunk. Fractals do not define quantity (for example, the number of meters), but quality (the boundaries of the shape).

We can build on the nature of fractal structures to generate an organization that can change direction quickly. In a business in which self-similarity of values and beliefs has emerged at all levels and in all geographic areas, effective teams can be assembled very quickly to take advantage of sudden opportunities or handle unexpected threats. The complexity advantage steps for success (see Chapter 7) can be used to grow an effective business culture and a set of processes that are fractal.

Concept 5: Co-evolution

Evolution is the theory that those species survive that are most capable of adapting to the environment as it changes over time. To this familiar notion, complexity adds an emphasis on the continual interaction among complex systems. Each system forms a part of the environment for all other systems. In a rapidly changing global market, for example, the actions of one company (department or team) trigger actions and reactions in other companies (departments or teams), whose actions trigger responsive actions in the first.

The importance of this simultaneous and continuous change is noted by the addition of *co-* to the word *evolution*. Co-evolution is the reason companies today must run as fast as they can just to maintain their current positions.

Concept 6: The Four Natural Elements in Human Group Behavior

When human beings get together in groups, our activity is affected by individual preferences. Each of us is an open system. As Jung (or more recently Myers and Briggs) tells us, we distinguish ourselves by how we get our energy and information about the environment as well as by the information we use to make our conscious or unconscious choices for interaction with that environment. We use the yin-yang symbol to remind us of the richness and variety in human beings. When a web of diverse agents works together in a group, we co-evolve.

Group self-organization enables a unity to emerge from our diversity (see Figure 2.4).

Group behavior, therefore, depends on our individual preferences and resultant history, as well as on our common environment and collective history. The overall result emerges from four basic elements:

1. When one individual meets another, there are three courses of action available: compete, collaborate, or walk away. Competition and collaboration create energy. When a group forms, individuals in it will exchange energy that ranges from collaborative to competitive.

2. As unique individuals, we all perceive things just a bit differently from one another. As a group, how much and how fast we learn together is based on the extent to which we are able to share perceptions. The manner in which sharing occurs ranges from full and open to partial and very selective.

3. We make individual choices based on our perceptions and priorities. Group learning and collective momentum will influence alignment of choices—resulting in group commitment that is anywhere from very deep to very shallow.

4. The group's co-evolution will, therefore, be overt, explicit, and coordinated or covert, on the fly, and disjointed.

Figure 2.5 shows the four natural elements.

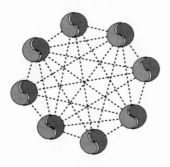

FIGURE 2.4
Emerging Group Self-Organization.

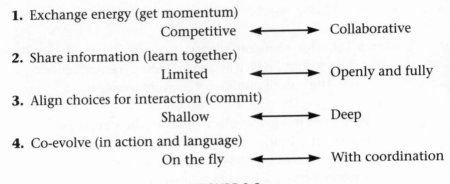

1. Exchange energy (get momentum)

Competitive ←————→ Collaborative

2. Share information (learn together)

Limited ←————→ Openly and fully

3. Align choices for interaction (commit)

Shallow ←————→ Deep

4. Co-evolve (in action and language)

On the fly ←————→ With coordination

FIGURE 2.5
**The Continua for the Four Natural Elements
of Human Group Behavior.**

Just as with individuals, work teams will develop behavioral patterns. Those teams that understand their patterns and maintain an awareness of them are better able to adapt to a variety of circumstances—changing their style when it is more effective to do so.

The Complexity Advantage Business Team: Working in a Natural Hierarchy

In a complexity advantage business, there are four roles—with a mix of old and new functional titles—that people assume for influencing positive self-organization:

- *Autonomous agent. A thinking, conscious, decision-making human being who makes decisions and takes responsibility for those decisions.*

- *Leader. An autonomous agent who is responsible for consolidating a vision, generating energy behind and boundaries around that vision, as well as encouraging an open communication and a robust decision-making network to realize it. (We do not use the word* manager, *because direct command-and-control management is incongruous with self-organizing systems.)*

- **Catalyst.** *Using specific triggers and expertise, a business catalyst increases the rate of change within a specific business or team context. Effective business catalysts can enable large and small organizations to self-reorganize to gain the full complexity advantage.*

- **Eco-technician.** *With expertise in mathematics, nonlinear thinking, self-organization, and computer-based modeling, eco-technicians help us to find patterns of interaction that might otherwise not be visible to us. They help us develop probabilities for future scenarios based on co-evolving patterns.*

Nested Systems and "Power" Hierarchies

We also make a distinction between nested systems and power hierarchies. Smaller or *micro*systems (teams) interact to form more *macro*systems (departments). Intrasystem networks will emerge in any group for communicating, allocating time and other resources, decision making, and maintaining focus. Connections emerge because they are useful and *used*—just as muscle gets stronger from repeated use. Leaders also emerge at pivotal or key points in that network. Effective leaders will naturally be selected by colleagues for direction at times when their expertise is needed.

Business hierarchies are more frequently biased toward power than needed expertise. The power hierarchy can become destructive when a leader's position and power becomes fixed and protected from a process of autonomous agent influence and selection. Protected power permits designated leaders to act for personal rather than system advantage. Effective self-organizing businesses recognize this destructive pattern and work against it.

Business Performance and the Fitness Landscape

As complexity scientists began applying evolutionary concepts to a wide range of self-organizing systems, new models were needed. Business fitness, for example, might be judged in a number of ways, such as by profitability, return on investment, ability to compete in changing circumstances, customer satisfaction and repeat business, and longevity and sustainability. Complexity mathematicians have developed a representation of the comparative fitness of a number of competing systems in a specific environment at a point in time—called a *fitness landscape*. In Chapter 3, we discuss the tools for looking at the fitness of your business from a landscape perspective.

Chapter Three

Developing Competitive Fitness

Internal and External Fitness

Just as individual animals and various species compete for survival, businesses compete for survival as enterprises and industries. Fitness can be measured in two ways, as shown in Figure 3.1.

> First, looking within the entity, by its ability to self-organize internally quickly and effectively in the face of change. Ability ranges from (1) ineffective self-organization that freezes a business in place, through (3) an ability to keep pace with today's rapid rate of change but not to lead this change, and culminates in (5) an ability to reorganize much faster than others.

> Second, looking externally, by the adaptation an entity exhibits within its changing context. The type and level of adaptation determines the success and, therefore, life of the structure. Status in this area ranges from (1) being endangered due to total adaptation for a context that no longer exists, through (3) being well suited to today's environment, to (5) shaping the environment by creating major shifts in the ecology.

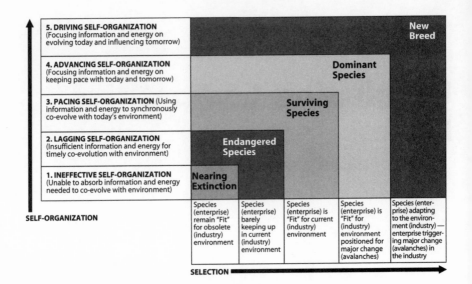

FIGURE 3.1
Stages of Fitness for Co-evolution.

And, as one entity is changing, so are all the others: those recognized as important features of the landscape, and those ignored, or unseen newcomers to the ecology, which may drastically alter competition for survival.

Identifying, Assessing, and Improving Your Organization's Co-evolutionary Fitness

To see where you and your business stand on a business evolutionary fitness chart, you must evaluate both your internal self-organization capability and the external selection status. Businesses self-organize because they respond to new information—triggered by events that originate both outside and inside the company. A business responds, for example, not only to events from the outside, such as new products or services introduced by competitors and changes in customer needs, but also to events from the inside, such as innovations in potential products and services and changes in the skills and expectations of its employees.

A Leader's Quick Reference Guide to Nested Levels of Corporate Self-Organization

The fastest way to grasp nested self-organization on a practical basis is to look at an example you already understand intuitively. In this section we provide two quick reference charts:

- *The first shows the nested levels of organization in human beings.*
- *The second lists comparable levels in a business enterprise.*

Based on our experience, we expect that—although you may not have thought of human beings as nested self-organizing systems before—you will find Table 3.1 intuitive and easy to understand.

Each level is, in and of itself, a system. And, each is located—or nested—in a larger, more complex level. The incredible profusion of different plants and animals on Earth has emerged in part from the self-reorganization of the surprisingly simple set of four nitrogenous bases in DNA. Through a variety of chemical combinations using very simple rules, genes, composed of DNA, provide a blueprint both for human cell replacement and varied reproduction in descendants.

A whole human being is composed of many nested systems, with cells being the smallest independent part. Human cells are capable of functioning independently but also self-organize into increasingly complex subsystems (such as circulatory, digestive, and nervous), which also self-organize to generate the whole. We humans do not command and control the billions of interactions that take place daily in our bodies to metabolize food, replace dying cells, or remove oxygen from the air. Nor did we, as children becoming adults, direct our bones to grow longer—although those of us who are short and wanted to be basketball players or dancers might have tried to do so. The whole system—the human being—organizes itself using genes as replicators.

Because we are conscious, we can learn to affect some of our parts and subsystems, for example, exercising a muscle to make it stronger, learning a new physical or mental skill, or reducing stress through deep breathing. No matter how much we learn, however, we

TABLE 3.1
Self-Organization Quick Reference Chart: Human Beings

Organization	Underlying Chemistry (DNA)	Replicators (Genes)	Smallest Independent Part (Cells)	Intermediate Organization of Parts (Mind/Body Systems)	The Whole (Human Being)
Hierarchical System	Molecules that carry chemical patterns to define the commonality or diversification of cells.	Units of heredity in cell nucleus, which replicate characteristics and functions in cells.	Simplest structural aggregate of living matter able to function as a unit and to regenerate and reproduce.	Cells, bound by common DNA and cell-specific structure, to form organs and fluids that collaborate to meet a common purpose.	Mind/body systems bound by autopoiesis; acting together to survive as a whole individual.
Nested Complex Structures	Result of closed autocatalytic loop in open system (DNA creates proteins, which create DNA, which creates proteins . . .). Surviving DNA molecules are the result of evolution and, therefore, reflect history.	In reproduction (during cell division), genes are used to maintain and disseminate a structural pattern.	Mutable over multiple lifetimes, cells evolve (change through variability and symmetry breaking) to meet needs created by environment.	Using messages and balancing feedback, system structural coupling supports self-regulating processes (e.g., circulatory and immune).	In turn, through language, a human being may structurally couple with others as a part of an enterprise.

simply are not capable of consciously directing all of the parts and subsystems all of the time.

Just like human beings, business enterprises emerge from the self-organization of their parts. Just as cells are the smallest independent parts of human beings, human beings—in their roles as employees, customers, suppliers, and shareholders—are the smallest independent parts of business. With people as the basic parts, business enterprise systems are much more complex than any single human being. And, contrary to what we may have thought in the past, the billions of interactions in the business enterprise cannot be consciously constructed and controlled by leaders, entrepreneurs, and managers.

Table 3.2, a quick reference guide to the major levels of enterprise self-organization, provides an effective way of identifying key levels of organization within your business. These points are—not incidentally—also key intervention points at which the effects of your leadership time and attention will be significantly multiplied.

In businesses, human behavioral "chemistry" is evident in the ways we interact with our environment. Just as there are four nitrogen bases in our chemical DNA, there are four preferences driving our behavioral network of activity (BNA)—the ways in which we, as individual human beings, interact with our environment. Our behavioral network of activity is based on:

1. The sources of energy behind our behavior
2. The methods we use to gather information
3. The techniques we use to make choices and
4. The ways in which we prefer to engage and change with our environment as it continuously evolves

Complexity science labels this process of continuous and interactive change *co-evolution*.

Just as common DNA in genes defines diverse cells that can work together within a human body as well as produce varied offspring, an enterprise's behavioral network of activity (BNA) enables diverse people to work together in a business as well as to create new businesses and opportunities. Memes are coherent patterns of human thought, which are quickly conveyed to others and which are easily put into use by those

TABLE 3.2
Self-Organization Quick Reference Chart: Businesses

Organization	Underlying Chemistry (Individual Preferences)	Transmitters (Memes)	Smallest Independent Part (Human Beings: Employees and Stakeholders)	Midlevel Organization of Parts (Teams: Work Groups, Departments, Divisions)	The Whole (The Enterprise)
Hierarchical System	Basic human behavioral patterns that shape the information attended to and the processes used for interacting with the environment.	Agent-shared ideas, beliefs, habits, and morals that propagate emergent enterprise characteristics.	Human beings, who can learn and grow to meet enterprise goals (and sometimes change those goals).	Agents bound by shared memes, team structure, and core competencies, collaborating to meet a common purpose.	Physical and virtual groups bound by culture, acting to meet goals.
Nested Complex Structures	Preferences define the underlying commonality and diversity of agents.	Through widely varying feedback loops, memes maintain and transmit group behavior patterns.	Employees evolve during their lifetimes (changed by experience), adjusting to changes in the environment.	Through communications and both amplifying and balancing feedback, the team structure creates a self-regulating process.	Preferably to meet constructive goals using win/win.

receiving them. Sir Richard Dawkins coined the word *meme,* similar to, and based on, the word *gene,* to describe a basic replicator of cultural ideas and norms. Memes make it possible to transmit—either consciously or unconsciously—patterns of thought. Examples of memes include the vision embodied in an effective strategy statement for a particular business, the compelling ideas associated with total quality management, or even the creed of the global ecology movement. Those who learn how to make use of existing memes or encourage the self-organization of new ones will be able to move their businesses quickly along strategic paths—without trying to command and control every person and transaction on the way.

The midlevel subsystems in a business are, of course, the work groups, teams, departments, task forces, and divisions that make up the enterprise. Those subsystems emerge naturally from the history, relationships, and successful processes of a business enterprise are more powerful than those artificially constructed by a manager or leader. In Chapter 5, we describe methods that will enable businesses to clean up the problems that we call *vicious cycles.* These problematic patterns are frequently the result of increased uncertainty in business and the fear that accompanies it. Vicious cycles tend to be intensified by a command-and-control management approach. In Chapter 6, we describe methods of enabling more effective self-organization to emerge.

The next section provides a method of assessing and then understanding the context for improving your business's internal self-organization. We then turn to a similar section dealing with the external environment.

A Leader's Overview of Internal Corporate Self-Organization

Assessing the Elements of BNA (Behavioral Network Activity). A quick and easy way to assess the self-organization in our businesses is to look at the business or parts of the business from the context of each of the four natural elements of group BNA.

- *The first BNA natural element is momentum.* In this context, does your team or your business derive its momentum from internal competition, internal collaboration, or a mix of the two? Does your business become more effective with time?

- *The second element is learning.* Do you and others in your business contribute to group learning—not just sharing facts but also your feelings and things you've learned the hard way?

- *The third natural element providing a useful perspective is the way in which people in your enterprise align their choices and make commitments.* From this context, is the commitment genuine, deep, and, therefore, reliable? Or, is it coerced and, therefore, only surface commitment that will disintegrate under stress?

- *The last natural BNA element is co-evolution in action and language.* Do you and your team co-evolve with visible and coordinated interactions—or is everything chaotic, last-minute, and on the fly?

By using these contexts as a frame, we can observe the patterns of our own and others' interactions and then determine whether these patterns are as effective as they might be. We will return to these elements in the next section—"So What if Businesses Are Self-Organizing Systems?"

Assisting a Business to Be Consciously Autopoietic. Complexity scientists use the word *autopoiesis* to describe the unique set of characteristics that living systems share. The drive from within a healthy system to continue living is one of its clearest traits. An autopoietic system is a self-organizing system that creates its own boundaries and preserves and renews itself over time—goals successful businesses strive to attain. Business leaders can help a healthy business community become consciously autopoietic by encouraging it to be:

- *Self-bounded: able to distinguish clearly what its business mission and core competencies are—and are not—as it organizes and reorganizes, and able to draw into it and use the people, energy, matter, and information needed to maintain its boundaries and vitality.*

- **Self-regenerating:** *able to regenerate itself easily by replacing people as they leave and replenishing spent resources, and in addition, easily able to add new people and create new functions as its environment changes.*

- **Self-perpetuating:** *capable of developing a strong culture with a self-similar—fractal—belief system to maintain the essence of the whole as parts come and go. This is a culture in which people hold the belief that the business as a whole contributes to the survival of the individuals employed there and the employees, in turn, support the whole.*

Maintaining Bounded Instability After Conscious Autopoiesis. Imagine a team that starts out with five members and, while developing the same project (a single piece of software for a client), grows to ten members. During this time, four of the original team members remain on the team and one is replaced. Although they add resources and energy to the group, the first two new team members seem to integrate themselves without changing the dynamics much at all. The third new person does the same.

With the fourth new person, members begin to feel changes in the closeness of the team and its ability to communicate quickly. They spend more time updating each other and seem to do it less well. They don't all speak the same language; they can no longer take for granted that everyone will understand their acronyms or remember the team's experiences in working with the client.

With the addition of the fifth new person, the old patterns of interaction abruptly do not seem to work at all anymore. Everyone notices it and makes conscious or unconscious adjustments. Then, when one of the original team players is replaced—one who was particularly skilled at communicating—the whole team reorganizes, trying new leaders and processes, resulting in very visible new patterns of interaction.

The addition of the fifth new team member and the replacement of the original team member did not directly—in a linear cause-and-effect relationship—cause a significant team reorganization. The reorganization *emerged* as the result of the team's history, including the original structure as well as the addition of each new team member. Because the team continued to develop a single piece of software, the requirements for the development acted as a set of boundaries. The team restructured within this context.

Healthy self-organization cannot take place in a business that is rigid and controlled. At the other extreme, no business that is in constant flux can support a market. Instead, healthy self-organizing businesses exist in what scientists call a state of *bounded instability* (see Figure 3.2). One of the most important responsibilities of leadership is to trigger enough change and, at the same time, maintain enough stability that the business community is able to produce innovation and quality performance continually for a sustainable advantage.

Periodically, the effect of many perturbations over time accumulates, and the affected entity—the business—must reorganize significantly to sustain itself in the new context. This phenomenon is called *punctuated equilibrium,* which simply means that a system (in our case a business) seems to function in a "stable" mode for some period—then, at a point in time, gathers itself together and restructures in a significant way to meet the accumulated changes in its environment. Fossil history points out this evolutionary pattern throughout time.

A Leader's View of External Corporate Self-Organization

Where Is Your Business Positioned in the Marketplace? A commercial fitness landscape is a representation of the comparative fitness of businesses in a specific environment at one point in time. Using

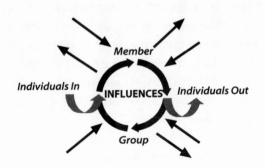

FIGURE 3.2
**Business System Evolution. Bounded Instability
(Closed Loops in Open Systems).**

rapid computing and graphics capabilities, fitness traits can be modeled in multidimensional space. Traits in a product, for example, might include such factors as speed of distribution, degree of product reliability, and percentage of customer-valued features. In a business enterprise, traits might consist of a rating for innovation, customer loyalty, average time from product conception to market, and depth of human and material resources. In a fitness landscape, each dimension reflects the company's best assessment of an important trait.

When a number of traits are graphed for a series of competitors, the result looks like a landscape with peaks and valleys—and so the name *fitness landscapes*. Any particular combination of traits might represent the location of a business—with very competitive businesses at the peaks and those in trouble located in the valleys.

Fitness landscapes enable us not only to study models with our best assessment of the current competitive situation but also to examine a series of projections—so that we save time, energy, and capital by trying only those scenarios that have the highest likelihood of success.

Promoting Structural Coupling with External Stakeholders. Over time, leaders will be able to identify those groups, such as strategic partners, customers, shareholders, and employees, that naturally have frequent interaction within the business community. When two self-organizing systems interact over time, their patterns of interaction become stronger. After many back-and-forth events, a self-organizing business and other self-organizing systems in that business's environment develop patterns of interlocking behavior. Just as developing the ability to hit a tennis ball low over the net comes with many hours of practice, the patterns of exchanged events between a business and a strategic partner become stronger and more established after many repetitions. With practice, integrity, and a supportive environment provided by astute leaders, business communities can develop powerful couplings and a shorthand communication that promotes fast, intelligent response by one entity to an event generated by another.

Synchronization isn't artificial or managed; it flows naturally from a history of successfully interlocking patterns of behavior. It is like the waltz of a happily married couple celebrating their fiftieth anniversary. Words and conscious planning are unnecessary; they each know the other thoroughly; their patterns of interaction are joined or coupled from years of experience. Each responds to the other naturally, instantly, and without the time required for conscious thought. Complexity theory labels this pattern of interlocking behaviors *structural coupling.*

Creating Rather Than Reacting to Change in Your Marketplace. Through the processes of adaptation and selection, entities may become increasingly fit for a particular environment. In the past, many of us thought that a high level of fitness—being at the top of a fitness peak—was highly desirable. However, when businesses get too methodical and fixed, they may get stuck on a particular fitness peak, become less able to respond to change, and, therefore, risk extinction.

One particularly valuable aspect of fitness landscapes is that they assist leaders in considering the benefits and dangers inherent in certain types of strategies. Tight coupling with a particular environment in a context of rapid change may not be the most effective long-term strategy. To improve their fitness, species at low peaks have smaller valleys to cross than those at high peaks. The plethora of messy but fast-moving Internet start-up companies provides a concrete example of a low-fitness peak strategy. Such companies can turn very quickly indeed.

Possibility space describes the range of actions available to a business. Possible actions are, of course, limited by the interactions, processes, and history of a self-organizing system. However, most enterprises do not even *begin* to include the fullest possible range of actions in building their scenarios. In the inverse of "what you see is what you get," what you don't see as possible becomes, in fact, impossible. We all need to develop the habit of fully exploring the space of possibilities, enabling innovation to match the changes in our environments.

We offer two techniques that leaders at all levels can use to expand their organization's space of possibilities. First, in response to the statement, "That's not possible, we can't do that," try asking: "What would have to change to make that action possible?" Sometimes, when we actually walk through what would need to be changed, the answer is "nothing." Second, when dysfunctional momentum or emotion is generating a negative label for an existing or potential situation, try asking: "Under what circumstances might this situation be considered effective or useful?"

Recall for a minute the software team losing and adding members, which we discussed earlier in this chapter. The team actually reorganized itself with each change in membership. In one of the more picturesque scientific terms, a change in a complex system is called an *avalanche*. Unlike the everyday definition of an avalanche, in the context of self-organizing systems, avalanches come in all sizes: They can be small enough to be invisible or large enough to reshape the entire system. The first few new members of the team discussed previously created only small changes, which were mostly invisible. After these changes accumulated, however, there was a self-(re)organization large enough to be observed easily. Even more colorfully, large changes affecting the organization of an entire system are called *catastrophes*. Catastrophes describe the domino effect in which one part of a complex system affects many others—culminating in a large change that affects many parts of a complex system.

Businesses that understand and use the full range of their possibility space are able not only to adapt rapidly to avalanches of change in their environment, but are also able to organize quickly enough to trigger avalanches that affect others.

Before You Start: When Changing Direction, History Matters

As a self-organizing system, the business entity both receives and generates new information continually. From the perspective of the business, each incoming trigger creates a response that, in turn, becomes an event somewhere in that business's internal or external environment. Each incoming event affects the system *as it has organized in response to all of the previous events.*

Every business continues to reorganize in response to its unique internal and external environment based on the outcomes of its prior action. The result of each action creates a set of initial conditions for the next required action. With this in mind, it is easy to see why no two businesses are alike and why what works in one business may not work even in a business in the same industry.

The history of a self-organizing system matters. Business leaders who ignore their internal and external history do so at their peril. Customers and employees remember the past; and, therefore, the enterprise collective is a direct result of its history. The existence of an individual and collective history means there is no such thing as a "clean slate" or "blank sheet of paper." The current situation emerged from a specific set of circumstances that must be taken into account. Any program or leadership approach in effect "pasted on top of" an existing organization, ignoring history as if there were a clean slate, will discover the power of self-organizing systems already in place. When we want to change direction, we must acknowledge existing systems to redirect them. Pretending they don't exist costs time and money and increases the risk of failure in achieving objectives.

Chapter Four

Old and New Models

WYSIWYG

WYSIWYG (What You See Is What You Get) is an acronym for computer screen displays of files as they will be printed. We live, think, see, communicate, and learn through a continually changing set of encoded abstractions called *language*. As scientific explanations of nature and the universe change, so do our language, beliefs, and predominant paradigms. Consciously—and perhaps more important, unconsciously—we, as individuals and societies, adjust our models; we restructure our lives, cultures, and businesses as well.

- *Before Copernicus. Our model was of a human- and Earth-centered universe—often illustrated as a series of circles with the Earth and human beings in the center.*

- *After Newton. Our model was of the universe as a giant machine, generated by cause and effect—envisioned as being assembled by interlocking gears.*

- *With the development of complexity theories. The emerging model is depicted as a web of "living," interconnected self-organizing parts that form a constantly co-evolving, morphing, and ever-more-complex whole.*

35

When asked for a specific example of complexity, we immediately think of the Internet as a good one. Although we can clearly predict that the Internet will continue to expand, we cannot say with any certainty how it will be accessed or used tomorrow. In addition, we know better than to try to control this World Wide Web. The best we can do is to go along with the evolutionary flow, looking for opportunities and climbing into convenient niches on temporary fitness peaks.

In recommending the Web paradigm as a useful model for approaching today's business world, there are two important points we want to emphasize. First, we are not in any way suggesting that old scientific learning from the macroworlds of physics, chemistry, and biology be discarded. Cause and effect does exist. If you kick a football, it will fly (one hopes) well down the field or between the goal posts. But this is not the full story. The success of the kick is not simply affected by the physics of your foot propelling the ball. It is also affected by the ball itself; the efforts of the opposing team; your relationship with the person holding the ball; and, consequently, the manner in which the ball is held, etc. As we form a network-based paradigm, we must consider not just the parts, nor just the relationships between the parts; indeed, we must consider both.

Second, because we believe that co-evolution and constantly increasing complexity apply to human learning, we fully expect that this model will also co-evolve with our "reality," or perhaps be superseded sometime in the future. When working with it, remember that it is a model—a method of organizing what we experience and think—not the world itself.

Practical Ways to Succeed in an Evolving Web

Following this chapter, we turn to a practical discussion of the complexity advantage, which is composed of the following three primary tools:

- **Four simple rules.** *These enable businesses to identify, undo, and redo their patterns of dysfunctional behavior, making it possible for them to move more quickly (Chapters 5 and 6).*

- **The complexity advantage 14 steps for success.** *These provide clear direction, enabling businesses to apply complexity science to generate competitive advantage (Chapter 7).*

- **The complexity advantage evolutionary fitness model.** *This describes a method for increasing business capability by using the latest concepts of evolution (Chapters 8 and 9).*

Complexity Science and Citibank: Understanding the External and Internal Environments

Most of the business applications of complexity science are directed toward the external environment, such as the economy, global market behavior, and forecasting technological development—or toward customer behavior and related delivery processes, such as production schedules or product development.

Citibank CEO John Reed's interest in chaos and complexity theories, for example, developed as part of his search for new approaches to sustaining Citibank's long-term performance. In the mid-eighties, he began contributing to the funding of the Sante Fe Institute (SFI). SFI is a private, independent, multidisciplinary research and education center, founded in 1984 and devoted to the extension of complexity theory. Their Web site offers this description:

> Operating as a small, visiting institution, SFI seeks to catalyze new collaborative, multidisciplinary projects that break down the barriers between the traditional disciplines, to spread its ideas and methodologies to other individuals and encourage the practical applications of its results.[1]

Mitchell Waldrop tells the story of the Sante Fe Institute, including John Reed's participation, in his book, *Complexity: The Emerging Science at the Edge of Order and Chaos.*[2]

> ... He [Reed] was wondering if the institute might help him understand the world economy. When it came to world financial markets, Reed had decided that professional economists were off with the fairies. Under Reed's predecessor, Walter Wriston, Citicorp had just taken a bath in the Third World Debt Crisis. . . .
>
> ... As dearly as Cowan and company wanted to see some of Citicorp's money, they also wanted to make it very clear to Reed that they couldn't promise him a miracle.
>
> ... Reed said he understood completely. "My view was that I didn't think we were going to get something hard and concrete," he recalls. He just wanted some new ideas.

Reed followed several avenues in his pursuit of these ideas, applying them primarily to the task of predicting the external environment.

As a result of this investment, Citibank began using—and continues to use—complexity-based quantitative models to better predict changes in the external environment. For instance, Citi reduces the financial risks associated with extending credit by examining scenarios likely to emerge in local and global economies. In another example, complexity models enable the bank to provide higher service levels at lower costs by staffing more precisely for evolving patterns of activity.

Perhaps an indication of Citibank's alignment with the new sciences is visible in words we use to describe the internal and external landscapes we must negotiate as we evolve toward John Reed's vision of a "Uniquely Great Bank."[3] You will recognize many of our key concepts in what Citibankers view as current key challenges:

- *Global competition within the context of a total world economy*
- *Increasing interdependencies, complexity, and rate of change*

- *A large distributed organization with set ways and territorial boundaries*

- *A need for cultural change, constant innovation, and continuous evolution*

By the mid-1990s, it became clear that we could leverage the lessons of complexity to gain further insight into our internal environment. It does very little good to predict the economy and prepare the perfect product strategy if the business itself is not able to use the information and strategy most effectively. Rather like a battleship commander who knows that, to be most effective, he must move his ship 180° instantly but can only make this turn over 15 minutes, a CEO may have the perfect strategy and need to implement it immediately . . . with a large established organization that simply cannot respond as rapidly as a newly formed start-up.

To apply complexity science to areas of organizational development and behavior change, we first took a step back and asked ourselves: "What is the problem we're trying to solve?" The answer: Many large and mature organizations slip into a sluggish mode of operation or succumb to unwieldy bureaucracy. Citibank didn't want that to happen. Many organizations seeking to avoid or trying to climb out of that dilemma had been using one new management program after another and had been less than satisfied with the results. Citibank was no exception.

So, What's Wrong with Traditional Quality and Management Programs?

Although many traditional organizational development and quality programs have elements that are very useful, the following problems are often inherent in them:

1. Many leadership and quality management programs were developed in the context of a mechanistic paradigm and reaffirm a reliance on command and control.

2. Few take simultaneous co-evolution of both the internal and external business environments into account. Customer satisfaction surveys and benchmarking attend primarily to the external environment, while the focus of facilitative leadership and self-directed teams is exclusively internal.

3. Scorecard and metrics programs often emphasize macrolevel stability and short-term results to the detriment of microlevel randomness, new thinking, or innovation.

4. Traditional programs generally employ linear cause-and-effect mechanisms rather than systemic coupling.

5. Programs ignore the history of the organization in which they are being applied. Contrary to some reengineering models, the enterprise is not a clean sheet of paper. Although reengineering projects might document current work flows in excruciating detail, they disregard the organization's true underlying framework of people, culture, and patterns of behavior.

6. Frequently, leadership and quality programs are point in time rather than evolutionary in nature. They momentarily jar the organizations they are attempting to help but fail to set up and promote long-term change. Working toward a fixed goal, some type of excellence, does little to prepare us for evolving scenarios and changing fitness landscapes.

Programs that neglect organizational context or modern world complexity and rapid change suggest partial solutions that won't work in isolation. Nor will programs work in a lasting fashion if built on top of dysfunctional habits—an unstable foundation at best. Some could work far more effectively if established under or aligned with the complexity advantage approach. By checking a program against the reality of personal experience and the concepts of self-organization, we have a means for determining the likelihood of its success.

Developing the Complexity Advantage

We started our work with the idea of presenting the Software Capability Maturity Model® (CMM®) in an easy-to-understand way along with some complexity science shedding light on why the CMM helped people to work together. Solidly based in the pioneering work of Deming and TQM (total quality management), the Software CMM is a very well-developed—though somewhat mechanistic—process model for a specific area: software development. We began by peeling back the layers on the CMM to see what made it work and—in a process of emergent learning that lasted over two years—we ended up creating the larger, systemic evolutionary fitness model that this book presents. Here are some of the essential points of illumination and transition we went through.

We first noticed how little attention was paid to the behavioral co-evolution taking place simultaneously with CMM or any successful process improvement. Clearly, it is impossible to apply a process model effectively without understanding how and why individuals and groups performing the process act as they do.

Next, we returned to a sampling of organic business models, popular in the 1980s. Initially attracted to their concepts, we had both tested them in real life and found them to be more popcorn than solid food for thought: fun and interesting but not sustaining. Our research surfaced their strengths: working bottom up, building in greater flexibility, and recognizing that unique individuals and their relationships are a critical part of business effectiveness. More important, we located the key elements these models were missing: critical concepts of self-organization and shifting fitness landscapes.

As intelligent businesspeople who are not physicists or biologists, we delved deeply into the differences between the old Newtonian mechanistic view of the universe (still very powerful) and the new complexity-based *relationship* view of the universe (even more powerful). Because we grew up with a mechanistic perspective, we spent much of our time integrating ideas of chaos, nonlinear patterns, complexity, living systems, ecology, and evolution. Concepts from both the old and the new sciences are joined in our metamodel of business evolution.

41

We drew on the techniques and ideas of several consulting organizations working within Citibank during our tenure. For example, BDA (Business Design Associates)[3] brought methods to help burned-out and cynical employees develop common goals and genuinely commit to them. And KLG Productivity Associates[4] worked with teams in trouble to help their members hear each other more accurately and assess personal behaviors.

We struggled long and hard with the appropriate application of scientific principles and mathematics to people and business. And, we argued over how to fit the concept of integrated planning to a rapidly changing world without becoming either rigid or wishy-washy.

As we created our model, we kept testing it to be sure it was consistent, didn't have any holes, and took into account the learning from both the old and new sciences. This process sent us back to research again and again. As the metamodel emerged from our dissections and extrapolations, we tested it against our own experiences, from developing business to software to even personal areas of our lives. For us this was a crucial test. Would the principles of business evolution be congruent with the full range of day-to-day experience? For the most part they were and, when they weren't, we adjusted the model again.

We asked some experienced business associates and practicing scientists to review the model. To our delight, they were enthusiastic but not simply accepting. They added their own thoughts and ideas and noted with acuity holes we had missed.

The Software CMM: A Good Base from Which to Start

There are three reasons why the Software CMM was a good base model from which to start.

First, it is one of the few practical, research-based, evolutionary models in existence. In addition, probably because it was so firmly rooted in the practical experience of software engineers around the world, it reflected the real world as described in complexity and systems theories and quite unconsciously described a process to promote effective self-organization.

Second, it was being used by real businesspeople around the world to improve their processes and their ability to deliver cost-effective, high-quality software products in time to meet customer needs. In addition to our own experiences, we could watch others work with and assess the model. It had the virtue of being tested for effectiveness in a highly competitive global market—with real bottom-line consequences.

Finally, we believe that most jobs today—and especially tomorrow—will be more like software development than manufacturing. In the Information Age, workers will be prized for their abilities:

- *To think effectively*

- *To observe and report important changes in local conditions*

- *To work in teams and coordinate increasingly complicated interactions with others*

- *To be dependable and able to depend on others, including those located in other parts of the world*

- *To upgrade their skills and knowledge of new tools continuously*

- *To engage rapid changes of direction in response to changes in the environment*

- *To produce meticulous delivery in a range of global marketplaces*

When looking for a structure that would help businesses to increase their effectiveness, the software development Capability Maturity Model was the perfect place to start.

An Important Postscript: Mathematics and Complexity

Early records show that mathematics arose in response to the practical needs of industry and agriculture in ancient Egypt and Mesopotamia (possibly in India and China as well), and that basic math (arithmetic) preceded the symbols that were to become written language.

Once again, the practical needs of business and industry to understand and make predictions in a complex global market are driving the increased use of mathematics. High-speed computers, sophisticated languages, and growing mathematical disciplines, such as statistics and probability theory,[5] make it possible to develop computational models that were formerly so complex they were practically impossible (see Figure 4.1). In addition, these tools help us to find the order in things so complex we thought they were completely without structure. This century produced two major trends in mathematical development: (1) increasing generalization and abstraction and (2) application to areas such as economics, linguistics, ecosystems, and other social sciences. Both support business demand for more precise descriptions of the market environment—a competitive necessity.

"I Am Not a Number": Mathematics Is Much More than Linear Arithmetic

When the protagonist of a frequently rerun 1960s TV program, *The Prisoner,* protested, "I am not a number," he spoke for many who resist—sometimes strongly—the inappropriate use of mathematics. Although

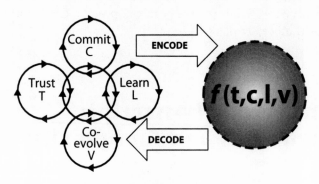

FIGURE 4.1
Nonlinear Modeling.

math, like any tool, can be—and has been—misused, this sentiment generally stems from a fear that mathematical abstraction will obscure rather than clarify situations being described.

Although most people today can read and write, fewer of us can do more than arithmetic and basic algebra. To many, mathematics feels hard, constricting, and Newtonian. When someone says, "I am not a number," we believe he or she is saying, in effect, "I cannot be described by a simple mathematical abstraction. I am a unique self-organizing system with a wide range of capabilities and possibilities." We can't agree more.

Using simple linear tools in complex nonlinear situations will provide misleading forecasts, a disaster for any business. More dangerous, however, is not making use of proven nonlinear tools to interpret and predict our complex environment—especially if competitors do!

Using mathematics to describe the V shape naturally formed by a flight of Canadian geese over a lake in Montana neither eliminates the beauty of the flight nor takes away the freedom of the individual bird to fly as conditions and individual intentions permit.

So What if Businesses Are Self-Organizing Systems?

5. What if Businesses Are Self-Organizing Systems?

Chapter Five

Surviving in Fear

Behavior Emerging from High Change, Complexity, Fear, and "Control" Management

During the last 40 years, the Information Age has been ushered in with avalanche upon avalanche of change. These avalanches have ranged in size from almost unnoticeable to large catastrophes—creating new markets and unheard-of business propositions. Before Netscape and Yahoo, who would have thought of starting a company by *giving away* its products and absorbing losses for several years? Technology changes have been toppling major corporations, triggering stock market collapses, redefining product design, production, and distribution, and requiring new and constantly changing knowledge and skills.

Technology has brought new meaning to the concepts of time to market and quality. A new chip in a device instantly transforms it— granting new functionality, speed, accuracy, or cost-effectiveness. Previously, new product introduction involved significant one-time investment in factory retooling, assembly line setup, and distribution change. Today, a new software product can be created and transmitted electronically to customers in minutes while simultaneously generating automatic account debits to those acknowledging receipt.

Customers, competition, and technological advances are also driving increased customization. For example, in the case of Levi's, technology is producing individually tailored jeans—tailored not by a person but with the assistance of a software program. To meet customer demands for speed, Williams-Sonoma and Federal Express couple to offer delivery of Christmas gifts ordered by noon Pacific Standard Time on December 23rd just a day and a half later on December 25th in the continental United States. Earlier this century, customers were delighted by a shipment carried by train and delivered in the same month.

Over the last 100 years, consider the avalanches emanating from telephones, cars, airplanes, packaged frozen food, credit cards, bioengineering, fax machines, personal computers, the Internet, and cell phones. These have triggered major business opportunities, instabilities, uncertainties, and upheaval.

In turn, change begets change. Competition is now global. There is always someone working while you are sleeping. New markets and business contenders are booming in Asia. New divisions and assignments are created to focus on these "emerging markets"—a term that didn't even exist 10 years ago.

Response has varied company by company (and individual by individual), depending on their history and status of the moment. A well-funded company, perched near the top of a fitness peak with a tradition of change, might embrace the new market opportunities provided. A similarly well-funded company, with a more rigid structure and little tradition of change, may try to control the avalanches through government lobbying and tighter internal procedures. Under pressure, less well-funded companies might position and reposition products, further confusing the market. The avalanches of the Information Age have given rise to a business environment that is appropriately characterized as *far from equilibrium*—a condition that permits self-organization.

Open systems self-organize, which means that structure and process *emerge* from the business history and environmental conditions. Business structure and process cannot be "commanded" or "controlled." Yet, armed with a Newtonian mechanistic mind-set and management pioneer F. W. Taylor's lessons of "scientific management," many business leaders try increasing authority and control to combat increasing market pressure, replace dying markets, and build new markets (see Figure 5.1). They continue to push logical, top-down solutions and repeatedly—under increased pressure—introduce new, flavor-of-the-month or -year programs. Strategies used in one instance and appearing successful or simply appropriate are widely replicated. Company reorganizations, mergers, operational relocations, restructuring, TQM (total quality management), reengineering, and downsizing or rightsizing programs abound.

In many cases, the results have not been what business leaders or employees hoped for. With delays in product and service development persisting, time to market has not been as fast as planned or, more devastating to some, as fast as the competition. Simultaneously, more informed customers continue to demand better quality. Employees at all levels, including the leaders themselves, assess the results of these programs and become increasingly cynical.

Some readers may wish to protest that command and control seemed to work well enough for almost a century. Products made it to market more quickly than in previous times. Customers were happy with the quality of their new factory-made cars and clothes. Despite obvious abuses in the railroad and mining industries, millions of managers and workers worked in comparative content. What's wrong with this technique today?

The faster rate of change has made it competitively impossible to continue a key ingredient in the old overarching collaboration between management and workers: "You follow my rules and I will guarantee lifetime employment." Working in a command-and-control environment may

FIGURE 5.1

Effect of Rapid Change and Competitive Pressure. Dysfunctional Environments: The Control Feedback Loop.

not have been entirely pleasant, but this basic understanding prevented the massive dysfunction we are experiencing today. Even if not enriched by their jobs, 40 years ago most workers could reasonably expect to be employed and able to support themselves and their families throughout their working lives. Today, even large and successful companies cannot guarantee lifetime employment. Many companies, themselves, don't even remain in existence. Among those successful enough to be listed among the Fortune 500, more than half disappear every 10 years.

Although companies are unable to guarantee "loyalty" to individuals in terms of lifetime employment, a command-and-control management style continues to expect traditional corporate loyalty from individuals. When employees don't fulfill this one-sided contract, command-and-control managers feel out of control and institute stronger audits, checks, and other bureaucratic processes—often making the situation worse.

Even more unsettling than the lack of job guarantees is the lack of clear rules of competition for winning the jobs available. When businesses close divisions, downsize, or move operations to another part of the world, people who have performed as "commanded" still get laid off. Sometimes those perceived as "disobeying commands" seem to thrive, even getting promoted. In a competitive free-for-all, self-interest and survival prevails.

The asymmetry of power embedded in corporate "power" hierarchies intensifies this game of internal competition for survival. Nowhere in our ecology does a natural hierarchy exist in which a potential predator (who can eat you for lunch) also controls the food chain and resources of the prey. If command-and-control managers demand compliance, they will get it—even if that compliance, in many cases, is a facade or, worse yet, detrimental to the enterprise. For the sake of supporting themselves and their families, people let themselves be coerced into at least pretending to do what they're told. Healthy risk-taking diminishes greatly: Suggestions and the identification of hidden opportunities or problems are avoided as visibility itself is often considered dangerous. People naturally choose to protect themselves.

Unbridled competition for survival provides a powerful momentum behind self-organization—but not necessarily a desirable one when competition is turned inward! Although fear does not *always* generate mistrust or deception, they are frequent responses to threat of survival. Even though the parts of a business—the individuals—may be relatively honest, the whole is greater than the sum of the parts; and a pattern of dysfunctional behavior easily emerges. One person may respond with a small deception, another by protecting his or her territory, and a third by agreeing to any request and then pursuing a private agenda. Undetected, these individual acts are reinforced and often become part of an interlocking set of closed behavioral loops (see Figure 5.2). Remember, the key to living systems—*the key to life itself*—is the natural evolution of closed loops to achieve self-organized order: bounded instability in an open system. Attempts to control them are as ineffective as a person trying to control digestion, immunity, and respiration consciously. In an emotionally charged, uncertain, and unstable environment, closed behavioral loops take on a life of their own. New work group structures and norms *emerge*. This emergent behavior may be quite negative—generating a "stable" business environment in which no one is happy. With enough energy coming into the system, a dysfunctional organization—like a pot of boiling water on a stove—can simmer indefinitely until it evaporates.

Dysfunctional Closed Behavioral Loops

We now turn to the closed loops that operate with each of the four natural elements underlying human group behavior. We begin our analysis

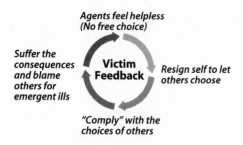

FIGURE 5.2
Effect of Rapid Change and Command/Control. Dysfunctional Environments: The Victim Feedback Loop.

from the context—or perspective—of our <u>momentum</u> and ask what energy is fueling people's actions in a dysfunctional organization. Let us assume that, although the situation will, of course, be more complex than this, the energy of the group is derived primarily from uncertainty and fear.

Having identified the primary energy, we move next to the context of <u>group relationships or group consensus</u> (parts belonging to the whole) and ask how do people structurally couple—or align themselves—when driven by fear. Research shows that, when driven by uncertainty and fear, people—concerned for their own survival—are unable to commit deeply to a group and, instead, organize their interactions in a competitive way. And then what happens?

From a <u>physical doing perspective or context</u> (*being* at some point in time), what do groups do when driven by fear and structured for internal competition? They limit possibilities for action, produce an unpredictable performance with frequent breakdowns or surprises, and lead individuals within the group to blame each other and other groups.

Finally, in the <u>context of change and learning</u> (*becoming* over time), how do groups maintain or change their behavior when driven by fear, working competitively, and experiencing unpredictable performance? As a group, they don't learn effectively and are, therefore, not as likely to co-evolve quickly to achieve high levels of fitness in the changing environment. To paraphrase George Santayana—who wrote, "Those who cannot remember the past are condemned to repeat it"[1]—those who cannot *communicate with each other* about the past are condemned to repeat it as a group.

We've constructed the following closed behavioral loops for each of the primary elements underlying group dynamics.

Exchange Competitive Energy: Fear. When individual agents or work groups feel that they must compete with everyone else for survival, they run on "us versus them" adrenaline. Agents, frightened of losing their positions, adopt threatening postures and tell "white" lies to protect themselves. Afraid to report the truth as they see it, they don't provide full and accurate information. Decisions, made in ignorance, backfire, leading to mistrust. People learn not to entrust their individual survival to others in the group. Mistrust amplifies the fear and the cycle intensifies (see Figure 5.3).

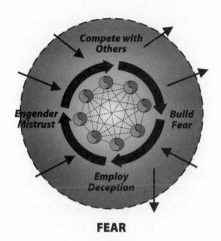

FEAR

FIGURE 5.3
Dysfunctional Closed Behavioral Loop 1.

Fear and deceit waste energy. In many organizations today, an intricate protocol has emerged for generating fear and spreading deception. We have both attended meetings, and perhaps you have as well, in which a manager issued dictates about efforts and the date by which they were to be completed. Anyone trying to raise valid concerns would be cut off with the comment: "If you can't do it, I'll find someone who can!"

The standard weapon being wielded is fear of job loss. What emerged, in our experience, was an ingenuous game of chicken devised and unconsciously played by everyone in "his" group. People who were otherwise honest and truthful resigned themselves to a pattern of deceit for survival. Here's the internal monologue for playing the game.

> The "boss" set the date. So, being the "little guy," I'll devise a plan that shows how my part will be done according to his time frame. Then I'll work hard to do what really needs to get done on my part to accomplish the real task. All along I'll update bogus plans and fabricate status that shows me running on time. At some point a major milestone will occur that will make it obvious the overall effort isn't on track. I hope it will be someone else who gets caught (since we're all doing

this), not me. When he or she gets exposed as delaying the effort, I'll claim the delay affected my work and add the time he or she bought me to my schedule. Over time, others will get crucified; I will survive and will complete my work on the delayed date that I silently projected all along.

Scott Adams, creator of the Dilbert cartoon, reports that he continually gets mail suggesting that he must work at the same company as the person writing "since he conveys corporate inanities so perfectly in his comic strip."[2] We find the same reaction to a description of the chicken game. In classes we teach both inside and outside of Citibank, we talk about playing chicken. People laugh nervously. They recognize the game. They admit to playing it. In the course of conducting training, Susanne was able to watch the patterns of people and their reactions when discussing fear and deceit. Over time she built a scale of fear-based management and placed some key managers on it. Then, knowing the degree to which the game of chicken was in place in their units, she could track major software development efforts that were struggling with surprises and overruns. Correlation is high. Deceit emerges from fear and carries a hefty price tag.

By action and example, the leader creates the environment in which honesty or deception will most likely exist. When endeavoring to promote balancing feedback in a fear-driven environment, the major hurdle is to remove the underlying fear of telling the truth. Much easier said than done. And, just removing the leader won't change the situation; habits remain long after those who engendered them are gone. There must be an investment of energy to combat negative memories and customs and to generate new positive ones.

The second element underlying group dynamics concerns the type and amount of information that is shared among the members of the group.

Hold Information: Limited Learning. Because they feel insecure, people hoard unique knowledge and capabilities as protection. Agents make independent decisions and learn at different rates. Individual growth is not fully (and sometimes not at all) communicated to others. To keep this advantage, they are invested in protecting the status quo and in isolating themselves from others (see Figure 5.4). The only person who understands and can debug a critical but undocumented software program frequently experiences a sense of job security and has little desire to provide training or documentation to others.

Because the work group does not share experience, it cannot enhance its capabilities for more effective future action. There is no shorthand for prior learning. ("Oh, we've seen this problem before. Remember the green pizza night?")

Even though some agents may have the requisite capability, the group as a whole makes the same mistakes and must reexperience and relearn, slowing productivity. Those with experience get frustrated with the slower pace of others; those who learn the hard way will be angry and feel burned if they discover that others had prior experience.

Fear precludes discovering and sharing in-depth. Defensive behavior leads to censoring information about problems and performance on the job. Even though they may be able to identify it in others, many people are unaware of their own defense mechanisms. Even when leaders work to remove fear, generate an open environment, and are the first to explore their own shortcomings or concerns, barriers to sharing information often remain in place. Such barriers include personal egos, feelings of embarrassment, tendencies to avoid conflict, and guilt at being imperfect.

Defensive behaviors that emerge for self-protection, cover-up, and face-saving often become part of the accepted organizational cul-

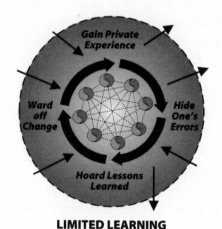

LIMITED LEARNING

FIGURE 5.4
Dysfunctional Closed Behavioral Loop 2.

ture in the name of team play, thoughtfulness, and caring. Although skirting the issue or pretending that it does not exist may feel more comfortable, the gain is short-term at best and fuels a cycle that avoids dealing with real concerns or issues.

In software development, we often set two engineers to work to find potential solutions to the same technical problem. Obviously, only one solution is put to use. Rather than addressing the situation directly, a team leader might feel that it is less embarrassing for a team member if he or she is praised for work that somehow does not fit the requirements. The leader might begin like this: "The design you submitted was excellent. I wanted you to know that I'll be using Jim's design instead, but we'll keep yours available. You should be proud of your work."

The team member is now either confused or regards the leader as not having the courage to tell the truth. In either case, the only way to learn more is to challenge the leader's assumptions. Most team members will remain silent. Some, risking more embarrassment and discomfort on both sides, may try to engage by saying something like: "OK, was there something missing in my design that was included in Jim's? Did he come to a different conclusion?"

A confident leader might catch him- or herself and be able to provide some constructive information. A defensive leader will continue along the original path, with phrases similar to: "Oh no, it's just developed a little differently. It's always good to have different approaches. I'm glad we have both options, and I'm sure you are too. Is there anything else?" For all but the most assertive team members, the conversation is over.

Humans generally don't want to put others on the spot or to be seen as negative or emotional. But emotions are powerful drivers of human action. However uncomfortable, sharing critical information means establishing the ability to identify, acknowledge, discuss, and sometimes change feelings. To overcome dysfunction, we need open dialogues about topics that are closed today.

The third element deals with the level of group commitment and the group's methods for decision-making.

Force Choices: Shallow Commitment. With individuals and teams divided by competition for survival and hoarding information, there is little shared definition, meaning, or understanding. Without trust or common understanding, the management-employee "contract" is further undermined. When driven by fear, people may feel (because managers have more power) that they must agree with them to keep their jobs. So, they agree to whatever is demanded—generally intending to do the best they can. We label this acquiescence *shallow commitment* (see Figure 5.5).

Employees can only deliver what is possible, and—driven by fear and competition—they may deliver much less. When they cannot deliver according to the original request, the result is a dissatisfied—and often angry—manager, customer, team member, or other requestor. Faced with this anger, people often agree to even more impossible requests—feeding the cycle with yet more negative energy and mistrust.

The manager continually feels blindsided by the delivery of less than was promised. Both "sides" are then dissatisfied and grow even further away from trusting and committing to each other.

To stop this runaway feedback loop, people in all positions throughout an organization must be able to say "no." In dysfunctional organizations, this takes enormous energy and commitment on the part of the individual. And, it may involve significant personal risk, including a potential loss of income. Of course, the "hidden" risks associated with continuing to work in a dysfunctional environment include emergent ulcers, heart disease, alcoholism, and drug addiction, as well as the less-obvious but more-pervasive misfortune of spending a major portion of one's life being unhappy.

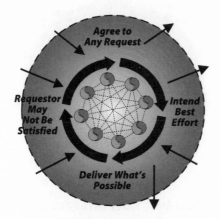

SHALLOW COMMITMENT

FIGURE 5.5
Dysfunctional Closed Behavioral Loop 3.

Finally, the fourth element concerns the coherence of the actions of the parts of the enterprise as well as the coordination of the enterprise, itself, with its environment.

Obstruct Co-evolution: Irresponsible Interaction. In a fear-driven organization, the planning process will be ineffective. Driven by fear and competition, agents seek power to control their own interests and ward off others. Less-powerful agents accede to demands from more-powerful agents.

This dysfunctional interaction limits the possibilities all agents will consider (see Figure 5.6). The space of possibilities will be constricted, with many ideas—particularly new ones—repressed either consciously or unconsciously by employees not wanting to increase their risks or give away their ideas to the internal competition. Management makes decisions about the course of action from a limited set of recommendations.

Not believing a fear-driven plan anyway, employees literally shelve them and, then, follow their individual agendas. The bookshelves of corporate offices around the world are filled with binders that no one ever looks at; the plans they contain were obsolete, too rigid, or impossible even before the paper came out of the printer. Because planning was ineffective, people agree without really committing to the plan and then do as they think best *without* notifying the team. Surprises

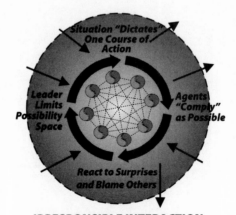

IRRESPONSIBLE INTERACTION

FIGURE 5.6
Dysfunctional Closed Behavioral Loop 4.

occur frequently—generally not pleasant—and coordination suffers. Because individuals are working hard, they blame others for the joint failure to coordinate in a visible way that works for everyone. Performance suffers as well. And, when leaders in frustration try tighter command and control, business work groups, composed of autonomous agents, naturally push back.

Vicious Cycles

Of course, these behavioral loops are far from the only closed loops that might exist in a dysfunctional organization. They are, however, the main drivers of group structure and performance. With sufficient emotional momentum, these dysfunctional loops establish an interlocking behavioral pattern (shown in Figure 5.7) and reinforce each other—increasing tension within an organization like noise increases the shrill feedback in a microphone. The patterns amplified by closed behavioral loops generate the configuration of relationships that in turn determine the essential characteristics of the organization.

Just as Ptolemaic astronomers created more and more epicycles (or cycles within cycles) as they tried to maintain an outdated and human-centered view of the universe, vicious cycles rely on dysfunctional epicycles, such as heroes, to support a stressed structure.

Commanding and Controlling a Vicious Cycle

In the last 20 years, responding to less-than-perfect performance in the face of increased global competition, many companies and executives have introduced programs to "take control" and "fix" things. Although

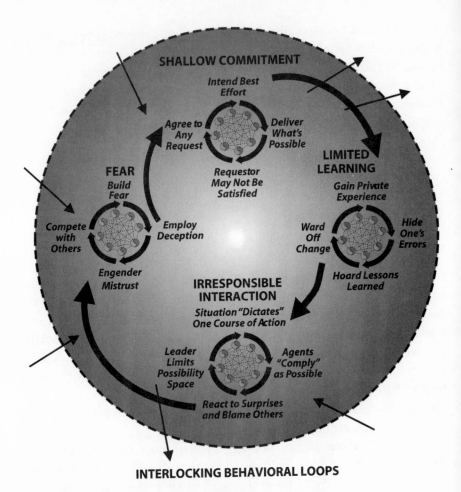

INTERLOCKING BEHAVIORAL LOOPS

FIGURE 5.7
The Vicious Cycle.

many of the ideas in the programs are sound, they simply cannot function effectively *on top* of a vicious cycle. Vicious cycles create partial knowledge and inaccurate information, which appear to be meaningful but are worse than useless.

Knowledge management or change programs become flavors of the month or year: a new one started periodically, with increasing frustration and pressure on the part of the responsible managers, and increasing resignation and cynicism on the part of employees.

Let us consider just a few examples:

- **Benchmarking (studying the competition or the best company in a given field to gain knowledge of a "benchmark" process or goal).** *When confronted with a benchmark, vicious cyclists simply manipulate the data they report against their performance to match the benchmark. We have heard managers say: "Just give me the number." Somehow, magically, that's what the results "are."*

- **Reengineering (examining processes and redesigning them "from scratch" using engineering and effectiveness principles).** *When the reengineering team sets up in the conference room and begins drawing those flowcharts that will eventually take up all of the available wall space, employees who, for good reason, fear for their jobs, resist passively and hide the real process knowledge and keys to success.*

- **TQM—total quality management (a series of techniques designed to provide products or services with end-to-end quality).** *When the pressure to produce perfectly becomes intense, people will hide knowledge of the defects. At an American midwestern manufacturing plant in the full throes of TQM, the employees hid defective parts in the lowered ceiling until it fell down. After repairing the ceiling, management carefully checked to see that it remained empty. A month later, the elevators wouldn't go down. The discard pile had simply moved to the bottom of the elevator shaft.*

No matter how good the idea, it has little chance of success on top of vicious cycles. As we have suggested earlier, a useful way of examining "soft" science programs is to check them against the key concepts from the "hard" sciences. Those that stand up may very well be useful *but*—and this is a very important but—before they can be effective, an organization must dismantle its vicious cycles.

To assist in dismantling vicious cycles, leaders may provide a positive role model, a supportive environment, and assistance for agents working toward fully responsible autonomy. They cannot command dismantling any more than they can command anything else. Some

63

people or organizations have expended so much energy generating, propagating, and combating mistrust and fear or other forms of negative momentum that they are unable to take this step without assistance. This has spawned a mini-industry. There are a number of quality consulting firms, including Business Design Associates and KLG Productivity Associates, which are specialists in helping people to make the change from shallow to deep commitments.

Chapter Six

Thriving on Trust

N ow that we know what vicious cycles look and feel like—and what drives them—we turn to examine the nature of more effective organizations.

Behavior Emerging from High Change, Complexity, Trust, and Leadership Influence

The energy demands placed on businesses and people in the midst of high change, increasing complexity, and global competition are substantial. In an environment based on trust, synergy and collaborative energy are high. Just as individual acts driven by competitive energy, mistrust, and fear can contribute to dysfunctional loops, acts fueled by trust, respect, and reciprocity help to create *functional* loops. What does it take to engender functional self-organization?

Writing one of the early human histories circa 400 B.C. Herodotus observed that "Men trust their ears less than their eyes."[1] Today we say actions speak louder than words. It is our behaviors, not our words, that contribute to functional self-organization.

Each person must become a fully responsible autonomous agent who respects the rights of others to assume similar status. Whatever anyone *says,* or *does,* no one can empower anyone else. Empowerment cannot be mandated through rules, bestowed by being nice, nor controlled through interminably detailed policies and programs. Becoming a fully responsible autonomous agent means reminding yourself of your right to make choices (see Figure 6.1). It means accepting the consequences of our own choices and giving up all claims to victimhood. Extending this status to all other people means giving up the idea that you are responsible for the choices of others or entitled to force them into actions against their better judgment. If you, as an individual, follow the four simple rules presented in this chapter, you will not only empower yourself and assume your own self-regulation, you can also provide a positive role model for others.

The next step is to join your colleagues in assessing your team, dismantling any existing vicious cycles, and then collaborating to achieve mutual goals and success. Collaboration means self-organizing within a framework of earned authority. Using designated authority or command-and-control power is less effective for three reasons: First, commands and controls absolve the commanded agents of individual responsibility; second, command and control sends natural self-organization underground where it is harder to influence; while, third, trust and collaboration naturally accompany authority based on earned credibility and influence.

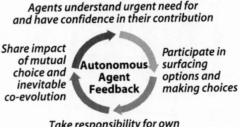

FIGURE 6.1

Effective for Rapid Change and Competitive Pressure. Functional Environments: The Autonomous Agent Feedback Loop.

Leaders feel competitive pressure but
recognize "control" is not an option

Synergy,
responsible
interaction,
and new
possibilities
emerge

Leadership
Feedback

Provide an
overall vision
that recognizes
permeable and
flexible
boundaries

Support agent autonomy and
collaborative momentum

FIGURE 6.2
**Leaderships for Rapid Change and Competitive Pressure.
Functional Environments: The Leadership Feedback Loop.**

Leaders concerned about dysfunction in their organization may despair at the thought of engaging all employees in significant behavior change. In Section 3, "Working in a Living System," we provide some concrete methods for approaching this challenge. For now, we offer two concepts. First, inherent in the words themselves, autonomous agents are responsible for themselves. Which is not to say that leaders have diminished responsibility. In addition to handling their own personal autonomy, their efforts are critical in helping to establish an environment of proper boundaries and positive momentum. And, second, although some of the individuals may not initially participate, critical mass can trigger a pattern of autonomous agent behavior without the active participation of every individual. Autonomy *arises from* autonomous agents who know they have a contribution to make. They participate honestly in making choices about how the contribution will be made and share in the responsibility for the result (see Figure 6.2).

Encouraging Functional Closed Behavioral Loops

In Chapter 1, we suggested that there are four natural elements that significantly influence human behavioral patterns and, in turn, group behavior. Those four natural elements of behavioral network activity

(BNA) are key to the emergent patterns and dynamics of an enterprise. Leaders cannot control or manage every element and interaction that takes place in their businesses. What leaders *can* do is exemplify personally a positive set of four simple rules based on the natural elements of BNA—momentum, information, choices, and co-evolution—and insist on them as ground rules for all team players. Our following four simple rules form the structural foundation for our business recommendations. Simple in description, the loops of healthy BNA are complex and evolve over time. But like DNA, they bring unity to a population of diverse constituents and richly varied structures.

Exchange Collaborative Energy: Trust.   To generate collaborative energy, we must make urgency and honesty the basis of all business interactions. This means valuing integrity highly and never resorting to fear and deceit. Deceit wastes time and energy. We all have much to gain by practicing trust and respect for one another (see Figure 6.3).

In addition to trust, we must have a shared understanding of marketplace urgency. If the business and its nested parts are to survive, there must be a shared concern that products and services compete successfully. Shared urgency is *not* fear. It is everyone's job to help stamp out fear: surfacing and eliminating dysfunctional coercion that con-

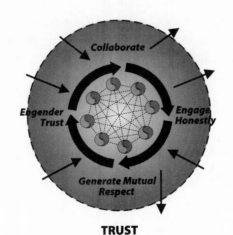

TRUST

FIGURE 6.3
Functional Closed Behavioral Loop 1.

tributes to covert behavior within our organizational context. In Chapter 11, we discuss methods of reducing the rigid designated power hierarchy while retaining an earned and credible decision and communication hierarchy.

In a team that functions on collaborative energy, people respect each other and grow to feel comfortable communicating the truth as they see it. By openly sharing differences of opinion and approach, the way is unlocked for the further building of trust. This is *not* the same as saying "make nice." It requires far more discipline to communicate what you really think thoughtfully and engage with what others are saying honestly (not what you think they are saying or would like them to say). Trust also includes reciprocity—a *mutual* return in kind of intentions and actions.

If all this sounds goody-goody or "new age-y," we want to reiterate that we are not proposing that everyone hold hands and hum, expecting miraculous results. But businesses can no longer afford the resources required to succeed without some form of trust. For those hard-line skeptics to whom this feels like utter fluff, consider the enormous increase in transaction cost generated by distrust. For example, every time a group's work must be approved or audited, there is the full expense of the reviewers, the time and resources of those under review, as well as the leadership time for follow-up. We are not suggesting that quality checks are unnecessary, only that, if your business requires frequent multiple cross-checks to ensure that the rules are being observed, then the cost will adversely affect the bottom line. The more audits and approvals required, the greater the expense. Team leaders recognize that the more they trust team members and the less time they personally devote to checking up, the more time they have to address new opportunities. Appropriate business trust relies on human capital. The value of human capital depends on healthy judgment and self-discipline, which in turn give rise to trust.

For businesses to evolve successfully, self-organization must be fueled by constructive energy. Successful businesses leverage both intellectual capital (skills, knowledge, experience, etc.) and social capital (people's ability to work together for common purposes). Without trust, detailed rules, procedures, and inspection mechanisms must cover all possible agent actions and interactions. In a rapidly changing world, maintaining appropriate rules, teaching and learning them, and then enforcing them is not only expensive but increasingly impossible. The cost and time to execute each transaction goes up with the number of rules that must be maintained. Trust is not a luxury for businesses competing in today's environment, it's a necessity!

When simple rule 1 is in effect, we can readily observe positive momentum. The work group's performance, learning, and alignment are energized by trust—yielding "us" synergy.

Share Information: Open Learning. Sharing with colleagues distinctions gathered through our five senses, insights derived, and feelings that surface allows the whole team to form their clearest picture of common "reality" (see Figure 6.4). Through joint experience, observation, and dialogue, people learn to understand their individual and group capabilities more clearly.

Sharing does not mean overloading colleagues with unorganized incidents. It does mean distributing learning opportunities to others and not retaining knowledge artifacts as a "heroic" power base. Conversely, it also means relying on others: admitting needs and being vulnerable. A group that learns to recognize and build on the strengths and identify and overcome the weaknesses of its members, self-organizes to produce a team considerably stronger than the sum of the parts.

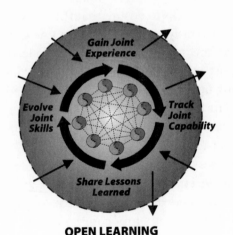

OPEN LEARNING

FIGURE 6.4
Functional Closed Behavioral Loop 2.

Sharing demands significant energy from the individuals involved. It requires time and attention to speak thoughtfully and listen effectively to colleagues. This process of joint learning requires a common language, openness to new thinking, pointed questions, and clear answers. The goal is emergent dialogue—in which both good and bad news is continually surfaced and shared—triggering enhanced coordination at all levels. The key is getting problems and possibilities on the table. The macho management attitude, "Don't come to me with your problems unless you have a solution," is outdated. Too often, recommendations that aren't fully explored become mandates rather than a useful part of dialogue.

Have you ever worked with colleagues that are champions of answering questions in ways that cause the questioner to leave and go away (as opposed to dealing with the substance of the question being asked)? We need to communicate in ways that support a meaningful exchange between customers, people making decisions, and the people executing those decisions. To function effectively within a group context, we must learn to listen to questions with our eyes, ears, and "gut," and then form answers with our heads and our hearts.

There is an old folk saying, "better the devil you know." The group can't fix problems that aren't known to exist. Another saying, "two heads are better than one," suggests jointly discovered solutions are often the best ones. Over and over again, evidence shows groups are smarter than individuals.

Human Synergistics,[2] located in Plymouth, Michigan, has accumulated considerable research comparing the effectiveness of individual problem-solving versus collaborative group problem-solving when those same individuals participate in a group process. In a study of 4116 participants in 802 teams confronted with the Human Synergistics' *Desert Survival Situation,* 81 percent of the teams improved their performance over the average of the individual scores for the team members working individually. We have used several Human Synergistics scenarios as team-building exercises in seminars both inside and outside Citibank for over 15 years and have been pleased to note an overall increase in the ability of groups to work together effectively.

It is not sufficient simply to share individual and group lessons about capability; in addition, the group must assess these capabilities against their internal and external environmental needs. With an understanding of the current and forecasted needs and their joint capabilities, people can then focus on the appropriate learning and other changes needed to co-evolve with their environment.

When simple rule 2 is working in a business, changes in individuals, their networks, and their interactions are shared with colleagues and joint lessons offer new capabilities for future action based on both past successes and past mistakes.

Align Choices: Deep Commitment. Make commitments that are both objectively understood, reasonable in light of experience, and grounded in personal values (see Figure 6.5). In the office, we tend to forget that each commitment we make is a personal promise to a colleague. Commitments require self-awareness and personal responsibility. This means we focus on both sides of the commitment: First, we don't coerce others into commitments they find unrealistic; and, second, we don't say "yes" and mean "maybe" or "no."

Probably one of the most important—and most difficult—changes for many will be the ability and commitment to say "no" when that is what they mean. In many companies today, "yes" means all manner of things. If people *can and do* say no in the appropriate circum-

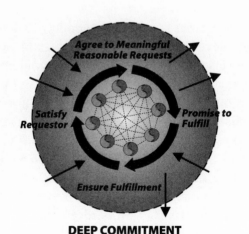

DEEP COMMITMENT

FIGURE 6.5
Functional Closed Behavioral Loop 3.

stances, when they *do* agree, this agreement initiates a dependable cycle. Deeply committed teams can count on the intention of constituent members when making agreements.

Should the situation change or a mistake be discovered, the new circumstances or situation are made known—and original commitments reevaluated—as soon as possible. If team members have not been advised of any change, they can depend on the original agreement standing.

To make deep commitments, people must have some understanding of what is being requested and what they, themselves, can do about it.

Step 1. Getting comfortable with what is needed

Step 2. Considering past performance, a history of prior results under similar circumstances

Step 3. Determining a capability—a range of results that can reasonably be expected—based on prior performance and altered by changes in conditions

Step 4. Using our past experience and dialogue with others to jointly negotiate concepts, directions, and approaches for a realistic proposition

While reengineering has been focused on process maps that flow materials, tasks, and functions of yesterday's manufacturing age, we recommend a model that depicts the nature of work in today's Information Age. Business processes cannot be accurately described as linear information flow but, rather, as a web of commitments among autonomous agents. The smallest independent part—and the most crucial for enabling trust to emerge throughout an organization—is the *person-to-person transaction*. We must all take personal responsibility for making commitments that we can uphold.

People often make commitments lightly with no real thought to honoring them. Although they say they want to be empowered and fully responsible, they don't have the habits for doing this. In the classroom, Susanne talks about making honest commitments that are "doable." Susanne's story:

I've listened in class while a student lists all the excuses why he or she can't commit honestly on the job—with the primary excuse being management coercion. As a class we discuss the need for people to enter commitments freely and the need, then, for each of us to take personal responsibility for our "promises."

As an illustration, on the first day of class I often ask that the students agree on class start times and length of breaks for the week. I tell them we have 8 hours of material to cover daily, the scheduling of which is negotiable. A simple commitment, no coercion. The class—as a group—sets the times with the understanding that a start time means everyone is seated and ready to start at that time. This process respects the time of everyone involved.

In most classes, the group tends not to be ready in their seats as agreed but, instead, to mill around until I herd them in. They wait to be told what to do rather than take personal responsibility for doing what they've agreed to. Moreover, they often "feel" there is group coercion whether or not it was applied. For example, in one class that had committed to a daily 8:30 a.m. start, one participant arrived at 9:00 a.m. every day. He dropped his son at school before coming to class. When asked why he committed—without objection—to something he *knew* he couldn't do, he responded that he didn't want to be the only one who didn't say yes. He didn't want to admit he couldn't do what the rest of the group wanted to do. He was unwilling to take responsibility, raise the issue, and allow the group to develop a shared solution.

While this may seem a petty example, it represents a widespread behavioral pattern in both large and small commitments. In many circumstances, it is a matter of habit. We urge everyone to take a look in the mirror: to reevaluate personal attitudes toward, habits surrounding, and regard for commitments. As with changing any habit, the first step is to notice what you actually do. Two definitions may be helpful.

Performance is the history of actual results achieved by an individual or a group following a committed course of actions/interactions (the game plan). After committing to and executing a course of action, what were the measured results? Tracking what one intends to do, does, and the results of that "doing" are key to self-awareness and potential for change in individuals and collaborative groups.

Capability is the range of expected results that can be achieved by an individual or group following a course of action—a predictor of probable future outcomes of that course of action. Only if agents and teams measure their performance can they understand their capability. If we can't or don't measure current performance, it is hard to predict what we're capable of. If we don't know what our performance is or what we're capable of, it is unlikely we'll make credible commitments. In addition, understanding our capability is a key ingredient in making improvements to it. We'll provide some further information about how to understand your personal capabilities in Chapter 10, "Autonomous Agents."

When simple rule 3 is in place, deep commitment enhances shared definitions, meanings, and understanding. Deep commitment is the underpinning of reciprocity.

The final key element in which we are assessing amplifying functional feedback loops relates to how a unit executes against agreements. Here we look at the degree to which the group is able to make visible and take into account its history when facing a wide variety of possible futures.

Coordinate Co-evolution: Irresponsible Interaction. Creating one or more scenarios for potential action and then acting according to the one they select allows a team to coordinate their action (see Figure 6.6). Effective feedback—both on the planning and on the execution—then enables them to be just that much better next time. Effective use of group scenario building—before proceeding—conserves team energy by mentally testing the projected consequences of potential actions. A group experienced in visible co-evolution builds its scenarios as game plans, using historical shared experience and modeling in a broad space of new possibilities to create the best plan of the moment. They understand that few game plans survive the game intact. Situations change,

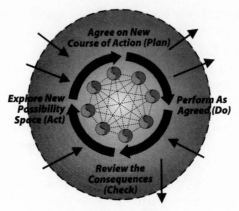

RESPONSIBLE INTERACTION

FIGURE 6.6
Functional Closed Behavioral Loop 4.

and making the changes visible (rerunning the tape after the game) fosters group learning.

Some people looking at today's rapid rate of change have decided planning is useless. We disagree. Rigid planning may be useless, even harmful; but flexible scenarios and game plans are essential whenever people work together. In planning, we make our intentions known: *what* our goals are and *how* we intend to achieve them so that we can align with colleagues and anticipate each other's actions. Having created a game plan, it is important we remain flexible enough to absorb changes in the environment. Continual scanning and dialogue among colleagues can rapidly surface circumstances under which our goals or means of reaching them need to co-evolve.

There is often concern in today's enterprise that too much discipline leaves no opportunity for agent creativity and innovation. This is due to confusion about what constitutes discipline and what is meant by creative and innovative work. It takes discipline to communicate changes in the way we do our work so that the larger group is also positioned to effect associated change. Until a business team is somewhat stabilized by disciplined interaction, people are consumed with crises. Discipline can help the group to manage the mundane events or thrashing of priorities, leaving room for innovation in the handling of exceptions and in the development of new opportunities.

The Shewhart cycle was introduced in 1939 by Walter A. Shewhart and adopted in Japan in 1950.[3] Since then referred to as the Deming cycle, it provides a simple model for basic discipline in the context of change. We have updated the rigid feeling of the original steps—plan, do, check, act—to take into account wide ranges of possibility. Regardless of what needs to be done, it is useful to cycle and recycle through the following steps.

1. **Set team game plan:** Design it to meet commitments and maintain evolving scenarios based on experience, information, ranges, and probabilities.

2. **Play according to plan:** Carry out the play according to the game plan, using and adjusting the appropriate scenarios required at the moment. Understand how this differs from the initially anticipated effort.

3. **Check (get feedback):** Observe the actual behavior that emerged, the changes in the environment, and the results that were achieved.

4. **Take action (adjust or continue):** Study observations; determine what you have learned that will increase effective performance in the future. Decide to adjust the plan book to reflect actual behavior, or redirect and practice behavior to reflect the plan book. (In either case, keep the game plan and behavior in sync.)

5. **Repeat:** Repeat the cycle.

The level of formality and paperwork associated with this cycle will, by necessity, vary with the nature and complexity of the work to be performed and the people called on to participate. All too frequently, those involved in planning get too focused on the format or tool to be used and shortchange the content. Some managers demand plans in standard format to simplify their job of review. It makes more sense to develop a plan in a format most appropriate to bringing discipline to the job at hand and those executing it.

When simple rule 4 is in place, teams co-evolve visibly and jointly explore wide-ranging spaces of possibilities for optimal performance.

Hypercycles

These closed loops function in an open business system to achieve self-organized order—or, in the language of complexity science, bounded instability (rather than chaos or rigidity). They interconnect and reinforce each other—allowing important functional behavior to emerge for effective competition in a complex and rapidly changing global market (see Figure 6.7).

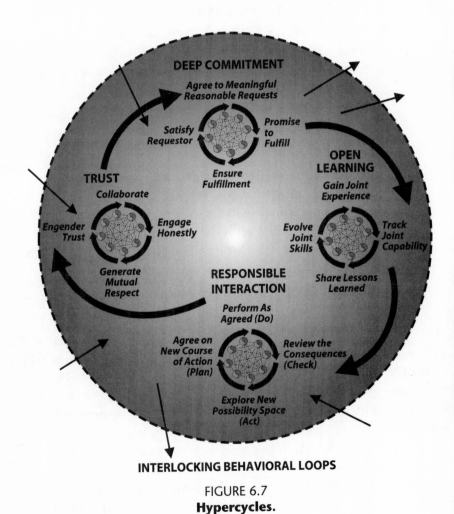

INTERLOCKING BEHAVIORAL LOOPS

FIGURE 6.7
Hypercycles.

With hypercycles, fully autonomous agents produce an emergent organization that can retain its unique identity while co-evolving with a rapidly changing, complex environment. New fitness peaks can be climbed, and increased competition can be met with collaborative creativity and speed. The handicaps associated with vicious cycles are gone.

Chapter Seven

Fourteen Steps for Success

I n these 14 steps for successful business evolution, we summarize the core content of this book.

Step 1: Adopt the New Sciences

The time has passed when leaders and autonomous agents could rely on a set of prescriptions as complete and unchanging (even ours). Businesses, enterprises, environments, and autonomous agents don't stand still but continue to evolve and to couple in new complex patterns. Agents who understand the concepts emerging from the new sciences can both formulate their own fresh approaches and evaluate the latest approaches offered by others as new situations arise.

We urge each reader to build a context for thinking, grounded in an understanding of complexity and self-organizing systems—to read widely and to test complexity propositions in the everyday business experience. We predict that the only way to succeed in the new technology-driven Information Age is to understand and learn how to think and work using the science of complexity.

Step 2: Create Urgency of Purpose for Sustaining the Global Enterprise

In an uncertain and rapidly changing environment, control is impossible; counting on stability is irrational; and living in chaos is an oxymoron. "Life" itself is neither stable nor chaotic. We must promote throughout the enterprise a deep and common understanding of the instability in global competition and rapid change. Making sense of the situation will help decrease organizational stress while maintaining urgency. For our enterprise to compete successfully, we need the full participation of all autonomous agents. Each of us must gather local feedback, identify opportunities and problems, and—within the changing bounds of the enterprise—make intelligent contributions.

Bounded instability enables rapid co-evolution, but it requires a continual inflow of energy. Leaders must invest personal energy in meeting the challenges of and tolerating the messiness that surfaces with agents engaging in overt rather than covert *self*-organization. As leaders, we must work at all levels to help establish and sustain flexible, semipermeable boundaries that enable, yet contain, this self-organization. Who "we" are and what "we" do will be clear and reflective of how "we" came to be, yet must anticipate where "we're" going and who "we" hope to become. Each boundary will, by necessity, be binding, yet elastic, simultaneously a buffer and a conduit, requiring a far different supporting infrastructure than we've had in the past.

In a world of software- or information-based products and knowledge-based services, the success of the enterprise depends on individuals who "handcraft" pieces of the product. There is a difference between standard products and a standard approach for creating products. Enterprise urgency and unity of purpose are important; standard products are important; standard infrastructure is important; imposing rigid standard process for creating products may actually be detrimental. The dangers of trying to impose standard process on a large scale include:

1. The standard doesn't fit with the local capability; or, in order to fit all landscapes, the standard is so abstract that it adds no value.

2. The standard becomes rigid and outdated.

3. When the standard doesn't fit locally, it encourages us to improvise and drive our actual process underground, where it is invisible and can't be monitored, measured, developed, or shared.

Within each circle of day-to-day colleagues, it is best for us to discover the most constructive way to interact among ourselves. It is useful for us to have a supportive organizational infrastructure, suggested options for working together, and successful practices from others that we might adapt in our own context. More important, we all need to be deeply committed to sustaining our own local processes and ensuring they are:

- *Disciplined, visible, measured, and improving*
- *Fluid, flexible, and adaptable*
- *Constructed in a manner so that we can use them to forecast and assess the impacts of change*

Step 3: Develop a Web of Diverse Agents and Visionary Leaders

Rather than a rigid hierarchical power structure, business enterprises are better conceived on a web or network model. Although there are a number of new roles important for the network—leaders, catalysts, and eco-technicians—the biggest challenge is to develop methods for using all the talent inherent in the workforce. We can no longer count on the knowledge and skills residing in a few key enterprise players. Thoughtful, accountable, autonomous people are the only solution (so far) to widespread complexity.

We are already engaged in moving toward team and participative management concepts, such as bottom-up problem-solving facilitated top-down by team leaders. The next step is to neutralize the concept of top and bottom. Granted, we have microdecisions and macrodecisions with different agents responsible for them. But all enterprise players are partners—conscious, competent, self-organizing across a complex web of required parallel interaction. We all desire and deserve equal respect and opportunity for coexistence. The concepts of resource ownership, power dominance, and abusive coercion get in the way.

Contrary to what some believe, enterprise change cannot instantaneously flash throughout the system via fiat; it emerges, over time, from the spread of new memes to all "cellular" parts and from interaction of these parts at all nested levels of the system. Biogenetic engineers don't "tell" cows to produce more milk and expect it to happen. They breed cows over time—or, more rapidly, alter their genetic makeup—for increased milk production. Farmers don't command plants to grow. They plant seeds, water and nurture them, remove weeds from their path, and shoo away hungry birds.

The prescription we are suggesting requires significant time, energy, commitment, and hard work. If each of us isn't convinced it's worthwhile, we won't take the necessary steps to make it happen. The opportunity to get away from the stress of vicious cycles will certainly provide ample motivation for some of us. The opportunity to thrive as a learning, contributing individual and part of a successful global enterprise is equally compelling. Sustaining urgency without creating fear is a delicate process.

Step 4: Count on Closed Loops to Achieve Unity

By recruiting diverse agents, we as leaders can encourage variation in enterprise sensory capability and memetic predisposition, thereby increasing potential for richer enterprise feedback and more robust processes. By engaging balancing or amplifying behavioral feedback loops, we can help synergetic unity to emerge from diverse players. The right mix of diversity and unity creates the bounded instability we seek.

Today, even when managers try to establish detailed controls for all the right reasons (increase stability, develop unity, and enhance productivity), vicious cycles often emerge. In the old deterministic model, the belief was that, if the employees followed the rules, then the company would achieve its target strategy, which, in turn, would cause it to become successful. Employees were not to think; they were to comply, and compliance was enforced by after-the-fact inspection. But, as many companies realized, inspections are too late in the production cycle to eliminate costs associated with defects.

Now, as leaders, we must not only put aside inspections, but also the concepts that were behind them:

- *Rigid execution should give way to flexibility and resiliency, the ability to change course rapidly.*

- *Thoughtful execution must replace compliance.*

- *A deep commitment to quality and discipline must replace haphazard production in the first place. Self-reinforcing and balancing behavioral feedback loops, not inspections, will enable all agents to contribute to enterprise self-regulation for achievement of purpose.*

By providing a functional environment, we as leaders can count on self-regulation.

Step 5: Drive Out Fear and Grow Trust

While most of these steps are harder to institute than it might seem, this fifth step is likely to be one of the most difficult. Fear is often the result of abusive power. In Chapter 11, we present a number of techniques for reducing rigid power hierarchies while maintaining a network of experience and influence for communications and responsible decision making. Neutralizing the rigid power hierarchy may threaten the vested interests of our more senior agents or leaders in the enterprise. Unless we individually understand the new sciences, feel the urgency of global competition, and genuinely accept these steps, we are unlikely to meet today's leadership requirements.

Many of us are older and—as we know personally—the older we are, the more arduous it seems for us to change. Fear may have worked in the old Manufacturing Age, because it was mitigated by trust in lifetime employment. Now, urgency is effective; fear is deadly. We must replace leaders whose primary tool is fear and whose unwillingness or inability to change jeopardizes the enterprise.

Recall the high transaction cost resulting from a lack of trust, which we discussed in Chapter 5. Saying "no" and constructive disagreement are two of the most valuable contributions we, as agents, can make. In an environment based on trust and respect, we wouldn't think of propagating bad data, because it wastes the time and energy of colleagues. Deceit, especially when multiplied by hundreds, thousands, or even millions of transactions, is a serious threat to enterprise survival.

As leaders, we can position catalysts and engage eco-technicians to assist in maintaining healthy ecosystems. All of us can participate in establishing self-regulating cycles based on honesty, trust, and respect. In the deterministic world of facts and reality, there was—or, in any case, we acted as if there was—always a right and a wrong. None of us like to be wrong; not only is it uncomfortable and embarrassing, it also generates fear of what others might think of us. Recognizing our environment as a complex web of nonlinear interactions and possibilities, we can eliminate thinking in terms of right and wrong. Instead, we realize there are many workable options and likely probabilities; so, identifying the most viable opportunities requires multiple parallel observations and perspectives. Isolated management decision making now gives way to leader-agent interchange and interdependence. Rather than being frightening, such interchange and interdependence can be exciting and empowering. It requires us all to be alert, capable, knowledgeable, and *independent* agents who have integrity and a deep commitment to discovering and working within the clearest possible picture of "reality."

Step 6: Build Commitment Across Stakeholder Boundaries

In this step we focus on functional behavioral loop 3, emphasizing commitment to extend synergy and connectedness among nested, intersecting, and related groups. Agent relationships and interactions give rise to the emergent properties and behaviors known as a business—*including* our nested and intersected relationships with customers, markets, industry associations, standards-setting groups, and communities. Dependent on the nature of the relationship, varied levels of commitment—always supported by complete integrity—are necessary, across system boundaries, for coupling nested components into a larger whole.

Boundaries are used by system components to help in self-regulation by containing energy and filtering information to prevent overload. Boundaries that stabilize the system too much become barriers that cause rigidity; an absence of boundaries leads to chaos. Either extreme is dangerous. Natural boundaries are permeable and flexible, allowing a variable energy and information exchange with the environment as needed.

There are a number of ways to build commitment across boundaries. For example, in their commitment process curriculum, Business Design Associates use a language-action perspective to highlight the responsibilities of both the customer and supplier in fulfilling the customer conditions of satisfaction.

Step 7: Improve Constantly and Forever Every Process Supporting Co-evolution

In this step we focus on functional behavioral loop 4, emphasizing visible co-evolution in a context in which agents are expected to learn and processes are expected to change regularly. We all co-evolve with internal and external environmental need. We must not only anticipate—but also instigate—changes associated with new internally created spaces of possibility or externally driven opportunity.

Expanding the space of possibility and modeling future probability with potential consequences are critical agent activities. If we cannot envision a possibility, it will never be; if we cannot envision ourselves working in that possibility, we certainly won't. One technique for expanding our space of possibilities is to ask "why not?" as often as possible. When it is assumed the organization can't work effectively in a space under discussion—when an agent or leader says, "we could never do that"—we must question the old underlying assumptions. Clinging to old assumptions in a rapidly changing environment can be fatal. At the same time, building scenarios and projecting consequences (from many perspectives) allow us to conserve our resources by eliminating (rather than trying) possibilities prone to failure.

We all have a dual-agent role in sensing and perturbing—triggering action among one another and the environment—our context from moment to moment. Precise five-year or even one-year strategies must give way to probabilities and scenarios. To function within bounded instability, we need a purpose accompanied by several probable outcomes. Making team intentions, interactions, and interim status visible to team members provides direction and feedback so that we can each see and adjust with emerging environmental conditions.

Through almost instantaneous electronic messaging and channel distribution, we have the facility for direct communication and collaboration among all enterprise agents.

Frequent leadership sharing of enterprise intent and progress influences and reinforces enterprise consciousness and memory so that agents are able to focus their learning appropriately and to act in concert. Agent feedback, learning, and creative ideas flow to initiate needed changes in boundaries and resources.

The course of action emphasized in the deterministic environment was control of finite consumable resources: material. Leaders focused on end-to-end production and conservation of material, aimed at sure schedules, air-tight plans, and just-in-time inventory: no risk, no waste, no messiness. Today, to be on the "edge," we must face uncertainty head-on and value virtual transitions, managed risk, or opportunities to leap forward with the environment. Systems are able to evolve and adapt to change most effectively when control is decentralized. Decentralization brings with it some share of waste and messiness. The focal point for leadership is no longer material but, instead, human resources and the generation of knowledge and discipline.

Step 8: Institute Open Learning for Everyone

Here we are working with functional behavioral loop 2, emphasizing learning. There are at least two levels of learning: enterprise and individual. We, as an enterprise, must continually learn from the equivalent of our species—industry and professional sources, models, and benchmarks that give us a more solid understanding of our enterprise fitness against standard. On the other hand, we must also focus on the experience and learning of each individual: our own personal history, performance, and resultant range of capabilities.

Enterprise Learning

Learning is generally defined as adaptation within an individual's lifetime. In Darwinian evolution, individual learning does not have much impact on species development. The Lamarckian theory of evolution makes use of a richer form of learning—when organisms determine a new characteristic needed to survive, they can "instruct" their bodies over time to create this characteristic and the resulting new genes and characteristics can be inherited by offspring. Computer simulations have shown that evolution is rapidly accelerated by such two-way feedback.

Without debating the limits of a biological organism's chemical makeup and the applicability of Lamarckian evolution to such living systems, we contend that we, as an enterprise, can and should make full use of Lamarckian evolution. Because our organizational complexity can be complemented by computer-indexed memory, timely data, and accurate feedback, rapid communication may take place to produce new memes on a needed basis.

Shared Individual Learning

When fixed, universal knowledge was the accepted context, formal training could bring everyone to the same level of understanding. In our world of complex self-organizing systems, formal training is only part of the solution. We cannot wait for emerging conditions to be encoded in formal training; we must also use timely experience, creative discovery, and observation of emergent patterns. This requires a disposition to learn all the time—not just in intermittent training sessions. Moreover, change is too rapid and time too short for all of us to keep up with everything that is occurring. Sitting in class full-time isn't the answer. Experiencing everything on our own isn't the answer. The answer is shared learning.

When we learn a lesson of value (either positive or negative), we must be able to share its context and results with day-to-day colleagues who are the most likely to face the same issues. If we, as members of a team, learn simultaneously from each other, we more rapidly propagate things that contribute to mutual success and avoid things that contribute to joint failure.

Today, many agents consider new lessons learned as their personal competitive advantage. For those who are part of an enterprise, a change in paradigm is needed. In business, we all win or lose together based on our joint ability to keep pace with the environment. It's simple: If 10 agents each learn one thing a week and don't share, it takes 10 weeks to learn 10 lessons. If we share, we can each acquire nine additional propositions for personal testing each week. Communicating our experience with others requires organized but unfiltered sharing (our embarrassing "bloopers" are as valuable as our genius).

Step 9: Do Business on the Basis of Synergy and Collaboration to Maximize Customer Satisfaction

Only by making deep commitments to support others, learning to engage honestly, and becoming trustful as well as trustworthy, can we build the synergy needed in today's global market.

In the 1970s and 1980s, Dee Hock brought a then-unheard-of vision to what has become the enormously successful organization of (competing) banks that offer Visa credit cards. A pioneer in the understanding of emergent self-organization, Hock founded a loose organization that established boundaries and built infrastructural relationships. Although few would argue with Visa's billion-dollar successes, many enterprises and leaders continue to be reluctant to release the old we/they competitive duality as the only approach. Make no mistake, businesses still compete for customers in global markets. However, effective strategies also include cooperation and synergy in the midst of competition. Win/win rather than win/lose can create a stronger market for all involved.

We need to place new emphasis on understanding how, when, and how much to share—including ideas, research, strategies, designs, facilities, customers, and risks. Potential partners for synergy include not just fellow employees and suppliers but others as well, such as customers, universities, government agencies, and, yes, in some circumstances, competitors. Long-term partnering relationships can enable that synergy to emerge, resulting in a system more effective than isolated parts.

In a deterministic economy funded by limited material goods, competition was the only response in the zero-sum marketplace. More recent quality programs suggested that corporations end the practice of awarding business to suppliers on price tag alone, minimizing total cost by working with a single supplier over time.

But today, enterprises have learned that they have even more to gain from vendors and others outside their official boundaries. In our current environment of rapid change, networks of vendors, academics, and even competitors are out there learning new things far more rapidly than we will on our own. We have to recognize the strength that exists in the form of partnerships and to leverage it intelligently so that we work effectively with each other. We must make sure that we use external as well as internal resources to stay astride of the change that surrounds us—that we are all able to co-evolve fast enough.

We, as enterprise agents, are not only parallel sensors, reading and understanding our local environment, we also continually make interactive decisions in parallel and take action in that context. As complex interconnections increase, we must all make judgments that consider consequences for others. When one person pollutes, it is, perhaps, no big deal. When millions of us pollute, there is a chance that we endanger all life on this planet. Autonomous agents have the choice of rejecting or practicing win/win thinking and action in our individual patterns of behavior.

Step 10: Generate Social Capital by Offering Employability and New Possibilities to the Workforce

Social capital has accrued when autonomous agents are able to work together to achieve common goals. Social capital is created over time and transmitted through memes: the belief that we can trust our colleagues, learned habits of reciprocation and collaboration, plus a tradition or practice of spontaneous sociability. Those organizations that can form new teams capable of responding quickly and without significant start-up costs to new opportunities and changes in the environment have developed a significant competitive advantage.

Using the four simple rules from Chapter 6, we can build an environment in which social capital emerges with fractal teams—teams that share the same attractors, that can be formed and reformed quickly at various nested and intersected levels. *Because* the players who form the teams share a common urgency, purpose, understanding, and visible method of working—reciprocal collaboration—they become self-similar regardless of team composition. Fractal teams apply the same core values and enterprise understanding to quite different challenges.

Two factors of the Information Age—the inability of most enterprises to offer lifetime employment and the necessity of many to hire "temporary" outside specialists—converge for new thinking about boundaries. With a little forethought, agent, enterprise, industry, and society (the economic nests) can all benefit from a synergistic blurring of boundary. First, although few enterprises are able to offer lifetime employment, they can and should develop the means for agents to enjoy lifetime *employability*. Were ongoing employee training and experiential development part of every employment relationship, all parts of the economic nest, micro to macro, would benefit. Each agent would have solid, marketable skills of value in the economy, and anticipated transition could be handled more smoothly. Each enterprise would benefit from access to competent staff and be able to change composition based on point-in-time need without causing pain or incurring exorbitant costs of unemployment insurance. Industry and society would have fungible resources. Second, we can enhance an already emerging global trend toward enterprise application of intra- and entrepreneurs. By sharing enterprise memes outside our corporate boundaries appropriately, we have the benefit of an even larger pool from which to assemble self-similar teams quickly.

Step 11: Adopt Statistical Thinking, Nonlinear Mathematics, and Complexity Models for Insight

To conserve energy, we must employ mathematical and computer-based modeling techniques that describe and statistically predict the nature of complex self-organizing systems. By encoding our reality as input to simulation and decoding the results as probabilities for the future, we facilitate rapid trial and error—a key to evolution and learning. A model is generally much less expensive than a market trial and can help to suggest those options to be eliminated before pilot testing ones that are more viable.

Developments in computer processing speed, graphic interfaces, complexity science, and mathematics have resulted in more powerful modeling tools and new ways in which these tools are used. Statistical tools are particularly useful in defining team or enterprise capabilities; parameter-driven models can be used to spot emerging behavior (trends); while computer-based scenarios enable possibility testing as well as mapping a unit's position on a particular fitness landscape. For full personal fitness and marketability, readers should become familiar with as many of these tools as possible. Large enterprises will, of course, employ specialists in these areas; but, as agents, we will be able to contribute more and exercise our autonomy more freely when we fully understand their inherent power.

Fixed certainty and precise predictability are ideals of the past. The tools in nonlinear mathematics describe shifting fluidity and probabilities. However, many people still associate statistical process control with manufacturing assembly lines and a mass-production mentality. In the spring 1996 *Special Publication of the ASQ Statistics Division*[1], Tom Pohlen provides a personal and compelling story entitled "Statistical Thinking," which is useful in dispelling this association. We are grateful to Tom and ASQ for permission to retell this story which, in addition to describing effective statistical thinking, provides an excellent example of a natural synergy between "work" skills and "personal" life.

Tom's wife Carolyn had been an insulin-dependent diabetic for over twenty years. Tom felt that by using SPC charts to plot her daily blood glucose levels, they would be better able to understand her body system and variations and, thereby, gain more control of her health and feeling of well being. They logged food, exercise, illness, infections, and stress. Tom plotted trends and ran regression analyses. In time, Tom found that blood glucose has a non-linear response to insulin—evidence of bounded instability. In short, statistical data has enabled them to bring some order to the chaos. They can now predict Carolyn's status with fewer blood glucose tests. Her insulin dosage has been reduced. Sick time is down and her energy level is up. The time between insulin reactions has been extended. Carolyn feels better!

Reflecting on his experience, Tom offers the following propositions:

- A system or process has no regard for specifications developed outside of it; it just does what it is capable of doing.

- Statistical thinking can be used to help us develop theories as well as test them.

- Tracking and recognition of certain types of conditions in systems help us discover ways to bring more predictability to an area of uncertainty—sometimes with powerful results.

Step 12: Encourage People to Take Pride in Product and Service Delivery and the Enterprise to Benefit from Human Capital

We must relearn how to apply common sense by trusting our own judgment, evolving our own thinking, and committing to the objective rather than the rule. Current bureaucracy robs people of personal judgment, common sense, and, ultimately, customer responsibility. Most readers will have had at least one personal experience in which a front-line employee of a large organization has said with resignation—and sometimes either embarrassment or anger—something like: "I'm sorry. I should be able to handle your request, but I'm simply not permitted to do so by (pick one) my management, the auditors, the system, etc." We need to eliminate our bureaucratic rules that call for mindless compliance that, in turn, encourages us to forget underlying enterprise intent and ultimate customer satisfaction. By wasting the intelligence, reasoning power, and adaptability of human beings, mindless compliance causes us to lose enterprise money and customers—not to mention the pride of those whose capabilities are ignored. Because the history of self-organizing systems makes us what we are, we never have a clean slate from which to start. Many of us have had years of training in how not to think or apply sound judgment. Creating an environment where we can all contribute good judgment to our work may be quite difficult.

Many businesses have started to remove the barriers that rob salaried employees as well as hourly workers of pride in their work and the ability to exert appropriate influence on outcomes. We not only agree but also see human capital as the answer to the paradox of maintaining enterprise stability side by side with innovation. Successful co-evolution requires that we rely on each and every agent's personal discipline, individual responsibility, good judgment, basic resiliency, and simple common sense to meet the needs of a rapidly changing environment. By applying our judgment, we will constantly learn and think about our customers that we serve, our environment, and the capabilities we have available today versus the ones we'll need tomorrow.

In his book *The Death of Common Sense*, Philip Howard describes the challenge ahead for those of us wishing to reestablish the role of thinking people within enterprises and institutions. In the context of United States law, law enforcement, and government, he reminds us that American forefathers created a two-page constitution as a guide to a distributed federal system of self-government. It was not detailed or ponderous but, instead, relied on judgment and collective reason. Over the years, this valuable resource has become more and more crippled by attempts to remove any reliance on it. Howard includes this story about Mother Teresa in *The Death of Common Sense*.[2]

> While on a trip to New York City, Mother Teresa was disturbed by the homeless situation and sought to help. She was able to purchase from the City an abandoned building in the Bronx for $1. She raised substantial funds for building renovations, put together plans, and proceeded to the next step which was obtaining a building permit. A New York City law designed to protect tenants from ill-intentioned landlords called for the renovation of any building this size to include the installation of elevators if none existed.
>
> Mother Teresa indicated that the cost of installing elevators would preclude her from moving forward with the project. She suggested that warm, clean housing and healthy meals were likely more important to the homeless than elevators. And she pointed out that the others who would live in the renovated building, Sisters of Charity, did not believe in luxuries for personal convenience and would, therefore, use stairways even if elevators existed. None-the-less, the city demanded compliance

with the *content*—rather than the *intent*—of the law. Mother Teresa was forced to abandon the project.

We all contribute to our society becoming steeped in bureaucracy and crippled by a compliance mentality that is destroying our ability to think, use judgment, and apply common sense in day-to-day decision making. Instead of a two-page constitution, the United States now has libraries of law. Governments and businesses continually try to be more and more precise, so that there is no need—or place—for judgment.

The more complex the environment becomes, the more complex comprehensive rules for interaction and the joint execution of tasks become as well. The more detailed the rules, the less room we have for judgment, and the greater the emphasis we place on compliance. As less is left to judgment, lawmakers also share less information about the underlying philosophy and intent of laws with those who will apply them. Finally, mechanical behavior emerges from the entire self-organizing system—constricting those administering the law and crushing those it was designed to protect.

Business or governmental enterprises cannot hope to thrive in an increasingly complex and changing world without active learning and thinking on the part of every agent who is part of the system. Business and government must restore the place for—and pride and satisfaction associated with—the use of judgment and common sense in working to satisfy customer needs and our own deep personal commitments.

Step 13: Seed Innovation and Harvest Intellectual Capital from Everyone

The United Negro College Fund has had the following as its slogan for many years: "A mind is a terrible thing to waste." Many enterprises do just that. In this step we encourage all enterprises to reduce costs and compete more effectively by using the minds they employ. To start, we as leaders must encourage out-of-box thinking across the organization and propagate an open, safe, and supportive environment for exploring innovation. It is up to each of us to actively seek new information, examine things from perspectives other than our own, and commit to open-minded exploration of possibilities. Each of us has the potential for discovering possible breakthroughs and initiating economic avalanches.

In the past, business focus was primarily on material as capital. Now, new creative ideas and unique knowledge are the main resources that provide the enterprise with an edge. Deep commitment to diverse agent perspectives, combined knowledge, and broad experience can offer significant competitive advantage. New approaches, adaptations, and mutations are key to ongoing variation and, ultimately, survival.

Each of us, in our own context, must take the risk and responsibility for mastering new and changing areas of expertise to ensure personal learning as well as make an ongoing contribution to the enterprise. In turn, we as leaders must support this growth by providing time to scan for, read up on, and think about, experiment with, and surface new ideas and possibilities for co-evolution. In an enterprise built on respect, open communication of thoughts and concepts can flow without fear of embarrassment and ridicule. People are more apt to trust their own instincts and commit more readily to new ideas or alternative ways of thinking. Emergent ideas can be shared, combined, rearranged, expanded upon with others, and supported in contained trial-and-error laboratories. The new sciences, computer simulations, and exploding technology provide a whole new tool kit for learning and growth.

Step 14: Sustain and Enjoy Conscious, Competent Co-evolution

In enlightened, cooperative co-evolution, all enterprise agents and appropriate stakeholders are fully engaged. Conscious co-evolution requires an understanding of varying fitness landscapes at nested micro- and macrolevels throughout the enterprise.

All agents share an urgency, understanding, and commitment to the four simple rules and these 14 steps. We know who inhabits which fitness peaks and how the fitness landscapes are changing. On all scales, self-similar yet diverse teams explore a rich space of possibilities and, through a web of interaction, work for mutual advantage. It takes tremendous energy and discipline to share freely our interests, motivation, talents, and information. The rewards are well worth it.

Applying the Fourteen Steps in Businesses Already Using Total Quality Management Programs

Famous for first teaching the Japanese at a time when American businesses wouldn't listen, quality pioneer W. Edwards Deming was an innovator who, unfortunately, was working without the benefit of understanding complexity theory and self-organization. In response to Newtonian theories of management science, in which people were essentially regarded as nonthinking cogs in a machine, Deming suggested that the people within that internal machine help continually to tune, redesign, and stabilize it.[3]

Deming's reason for process quality and discipline was to *optimize* productivity. From a complexity perspective, there is no such thing as optimization against a fixed goal. Neither the markets nor the business itself remains fixed. In the Information Age, business competition rarely takes place in an isolated regional economy. Even mom-and-pop pizza places compete with the global reach of Godfather's Pizza and Pizza Hut. Due to the speed of technology-driven change, by the time we get hundreds or thousands of people, in a global enterprise, doing something the same way (if this is even possible), that way is likely to be obsolete. Frequently, there is no time to get a return on an investment in standardization.

Instead of fixed optimization, we need as much pertinent feedback as possible to build our enterprise on shifting core competencies, and to co-evolve with a changing economic landscape. Product and process quality and discipline are still at the core of economic fitness, but must be balanced with additional trade-offs to help accommodate rapid landscape changes due to Information Age avalanches.

Although Deming was instrumental in bringing a more humanistic approach to management, he retained the deterministic and linear perspective of his time and prescribed enterprise success through optimizing process efficiency and stability. There was little excitement about what opportunities tomorrow might bring for replacing that machinery or how uncertainties could unfold. There was little motivation to be on the alert, grapple with hidden possibilities, or risk causing rather than warding off an avalanche.

The complexity advantage provides us with a drastically new perspective. Using the 14 steps for success, each of us can and should make a difference. The importance of patterns, participation, relationships, and dynamic connectedness is invigorating. Co-evolution with our environment suggests a new sensitivity, responsiveness, and potential for success. The opportunities we find in bounded instability give each of us a whole new impetus to think, make choices and commitments, then take action.

If you are in one of the many businesses now using TQM, Table 7.1 highlights the differences between the full power of the complexity advantage and Deming's pioneering approach.

TABLE 7.1

Differences Between the Complexity Advantage and Total Quality Management

The Complexity Advantage (14 Steps for Success)	Total Quality Management (Deming, the Pioneer)
1. Adopt the new sciences.	2. Adopt the new philosophy.
2. Create urgency of purpose for sustaining the global enterprise.	1. Create constancy of purpose for improvement of product and service.
3. Develop a web of diverse agents and visionary leaders.	7. Adopt and institute leadership.
4. Count on closed loops to achieve unity.	3. Cease dependence on inspection to achieve quality.
5. Drive out fear and grow trust.	8. Drive out fear.
6. Build commitment across stakeholder boundaries.	9. Break down barriers between staff areas.
7. Improve constantly and forever process supporting coordinated co-evolution.	5. Improve constantly and forever every process for planning, production, and service.
8. Institute open learning for everyone.	6. Institute training on the job.
9. Do business on the basis of synergy and collaboration to maximize customer satisfaction.	4. End the practice of awarding business on the basis of price tag alone. Instead, minimize total cost by working with a single supplier.
10. Generate social capital by offering employability and new possibilities to the workforce.	10. Eliminate slogans, exhortations, and targets for the workforce.
11. Adopt statistical thinking, nonlinear mathematics, and complexity models for insight.	11. Eliminate numerical quotas for the workforce and numerical goals for management.
12. Benefit from human capital by encouraging people to take pride in the product, service delivery, and the enterprise.	12. Remove barriers that rob people of the pride of workmanship. Eliminate the annual rating or merit system.
13. Seed innovation and harvest intellectual capital from everyone.	13. Institute a vigorous program of education and self-improvement for everyone.
14. Sustain and enjoy conscious, competent co-evolution.	14. Put everybody in the company to work to accomplish the transformation.

Chapter Eight

Introducing Evolutionary Fitness Models

Rome was not built in a day.

I n the past, we have sought quick-fix tools and techniques to deal with separate problems or parts of the business that changed. Unfortunately, these reductionist programs were isolated—partial approaches that ignored the complexity of the whole. Not only was Rome not built in a day, it wasn't the result of a single emperor or campaign. A quick fix from a single perspective frequently results in new problems popping up elsewhere. Leaders and catalysts need an overarching framework to help autonomous agents effectively address unique problems and opportunities as they occur. This framework should encourage the emergence of sustained, conscious, constructive self-organization. Because each self-organizing system is one of a kind, no single cookie-cutter program, process, or pattern will fit all enterprises or all parts of the enterprise. In addition—because co-evolution continually changes the competitive landscape—a program that worked once may not work again. The complexity advantage evolutionary fitness model introduced in this chapter and detailed in the next can be used both to assess business fitness and to evaluate programs aimed at assisting in productive self-organization.

The Complexity Advantage
Evolutionary Fitness Model

We want to begin by acknowledging that our evolutionary fitness model has its roots in the Capability Maturity Model (CMM). The CMM is used to communicate information and processes that generate agent memes for effective software development. Created by the Software Engineering Institute (SEI) at Carnegie Mellon, the CMM is the result of a very effective group process, which the SEI facilitated. This is how Watts S. Humphrey describes it in his foreword to the CMM text, *The Capability Maturity Model: Guidelines for Improving the Software Process:*

> Perhaps the greatest contribution of this book was in the way it was produced. Many software professionals from all over the United States participated in proposing topics, reviewing drafts, critiquing changes, and testing the result. The CMM represents the combined judgement of literally hundreds of experienced engineers from all walks of government and industry.[1]

Because the content of the Software CMM has been derived from experience, it incorporates the lessons learned from throughout the industry over time. The CMM encapsulates information about successful patterns of software development and helps produce a set of very effective memes. It provides a unifying language that has enabled thousands of engineers from around the globe to share data and lessons learned in a disciplined way. Based on experience synthesized from proven theory and industry leaders, it is a powerful mechanism for packaging and distributing knowledge artifacts to accelerate capability evolution.

Those familiar with the CMM for software will recognize in our model similarities as well as some significant differences. Although the CMM for software is an excellent start at functional fitness modeling, it was developed before lessons from complexity were widely accessible. It therefore has some drawbacks from our complexity perspective:

1. As in most TQM models, it assumes we are working toward linear solutions that are comparatively clean and can be "optimized."

2. Developed in a Newtonian context, deterministic language in the model describes cause-and-effect relationships. Words such as *manager, control,* and *certainty* abound.

3. It presents the world as being more predictable than it is. The fifth stage of Philip Crosby's grid model[2] (from which the CMM draws) is certainty. While business results are more predictable and less chaotic at higher levels, internal conditions and external environments are still uncertain.

4. The model focuses users on prescriptive processes and procedures with implicit rather than explicit human behavioral co-evolution.

As organizations use our model (like the CMM) to reach higher plateaus of competence over time, it is known as an *evolutionary model.* Our evolutionary fitness model gives members of the enterprise a structure within which they can co-evolve to:

1. Generate and maintain collaborative energy for alignment and learning.

2. Maintain a balance between *what* is to be done and *how* it is to be done.

3. Keep the focus on enterprise agents—their learning, commitments, choices, responsibility, and accountability.

4. Maintain agent game plans for action and interaction at an appropriate level of detail, consistency, variability, usability, and flexibility to enable co-evolution.

5. Establish a partnership between self-organizing agents accountable for the work and the appropriate support and measurement infrastructure behind their patterns of interaction.

Just as it is vital for each autonomous agent to understand his or her own performance and capabilities, it is equally important for each agent to understand the performance and capabilities emerging from teams and from the enterprise whole. Emergent capability is the range of expected results, which can be achieved within a system; past capabilities are used as a predictor of future emergent outcomes. While based on measurements of the actual results achieved within a system (emergent performance), capability predictions are just that—nonlinear estimations of a range of potential performances with varying degrees of likelihood. To build an evolutionary model, we add a new term: *levels of fitness*. In the complexity advantage model, levels of fitness are determined by the extent to which autonomous agent interaction is characterized by collaborative energy, deep commitment, shared learning, and visible execution that is scripted, disciplined, measured, and co-evolving with internal and external environmental needs.

Because human interaction relies heavily on language, the words we use to articulate our common realities are very important. The unifying language of an evolutionary fitness model helps order to emerge by rapidly spreading memes (stabilizing beliefs or language patterns) amid the uncertainties of accelerated change. Evolutionary fitness models concentrate on enterprise unity using common language, collective learning, and disciplined interlocking patterns (which we colloquially call *habits*).

Let's play baseball for a few minutes to examine two groups at differing stages of evolution.

Uneven Playing Fields: Little League Through Pro Teams

It would be ludicrous to pit the little league Mary Ann's six-year-old nephew plays in against the New York Yankees (or any other pro team). Much more changes between little league and pro teams than the amount of money involved.

When Little Leagues Start

Although delightful and sometimes amusing to watch, little league base-ball teams exhibit self-organization that is quite low on the fitness scale. Little league players have not yet mastered the basic skills necessary for effective team interaction in context of the game.

Often, an adult coach pitches the ball because the young players haven't yet mastered the precision necessary to dependably land a ball in range of home plate. The batter swings awkwardly at each ball thrown (whether or not it falls in range). The catcher doesn't catch the ball but, instead, scoops it up from the dirt after it has landed. If the bat-ter does connect with the ball, it ambles toward the first baseman, his hand goes up, and the ball lands on the ground beside him. Meanwhile, the batter stands frozen, watching in amazement as the ball he actually hit moves through the air . . . until the coach breaks the trance with: "Run, Johnny, run." On the occasion that someone miraculously hits the ball with enough force to propel it into the outfield, a dozen little legs start running in that direction and six little bodies collide as the ball drops undeterred, 10 feet away.

Player actions and interactions are totally improvised, unless the coach yells out commands that bring some order to the field. Left on their own, players make choices guided predominantly by reaction; pre-planned team plays are nonexistent or not remembered (except by the coach). While wanting passionately to win, many young players are so busy struggling with personal fitness, they haven't yet learned about commitment to the team and the nature of team play. Everyone is so unpredictable that others don't know what to expect. Undisciplined performance, unknown capability, uncoordinated player interactions, reactive trade-offs, and improvised plays affect execution adversely. Put more simply, they haven't yet learned how to contribute to, communi-cate well with, and commit to their fellow team members to work as a whole. Communication breakdowns are often apparent. And the lack of even a basic shared language has coaches shouting things like: "Run for third base, Timmy. No, *third* base. Third base is the other way, Timmy. Third is. . . . Never mind. Next time."

Because it is unorganized in the first place, the team has little capacity for rapid change; obvious opportunities are lost. Team perfor-mance is impossible to predict. Contrast little league with pro ball.

The Pros

When the Yankees are playing well, they are a joy to watch: poetry in motion. Every player displays personal mastery and discipline. The pitcher releases the ball not only with practiced skill but also with knowledge of the batter who will attempt to return it. Is he left-handed or right? Is he more skilled at hitting a fast or curve ball?

Based on past experience, the players in the field consider the batter's strength and the general direction, angle, or distance the ball will travel, should he connect. From the moment the pitch is in the air, the players on the field begin a choreographed dance. Everyone knows the part they are to play, the contribution they are to make in context of the integrated whole. Their physical interaction, triggered here and now by the pitcher's release of the ball, is a product of structural coupling they have developed over time, learning on the practice field. As the play unfolds, each autonomous agent co-evolves with his colleagues, the opposing team, the spin of the ball, the morning dew on the grass, the swell of noise from the crowd. The excitement we experience in watching self-organization unfold on the pro field comes from the precision and personal mastery we see coupled with the suspense, expectation, and uncertainty we feel.

The team's collaborative energy is reflected in deep commitment, shared learning, and coordinated execution of player actions and interactions. They work and play as a whole, according to a game plan that is studied continually and adapted to player, team, and environmental needs. The team with its support staff uses measurement, statistics, probabilities, and models to understand actions, interactions, emergent behaviors, and results. Individual self-discipline is evident in the action and interaction of each player. The team itself reinforces deep commitment and fidelity to the group approach. Grounded in the stability of a conscious team organization, learning, innovation, and change are eagerly sought out for the competitive advantages they provide.

In this organization, agent action and interaction take place according to a game plan. Game plans are defined, recorded, and continuously adapted by member agent consensus during practice and—by real-time reaction—during a game when new situations or breakdowns occur. With the use of game plans, player actions and interactions become visible and observable and, thereby, part of an articulated history and common reality. But plans are not static. Supported by management, players use actual results to update and change them—keeping them real and, therefore, valuable. To meet their common goal of winning, it becomes the players *themselves* who demand of each other that they keep their commitments and not generate surprises on the playing field. It becomes management's job to provide incoming energy and information and to assist in establishing a functional underlying framework within which to work.

ERAs, RBIs, and other statistics that die-hard baseball fans quote to each other are none other than performance measurements—both of the individual players and of the team as a whole. And when fans make bets based on statistically recorded performance, they are really predicting performance based on historical capability.

Through spring training and regular practice, pro teams have a disciplined approach to learning, getting feedback, for continual improvement. Pro teams know that a group of individual superstars, no matter how good they may be individually, will not be as effective as a smoothly functioning team. Through practice, players have the opportunity to make disciplined change (visible evolution) work to team advantage. Although it is true that the New York Yankees would need to make drastic changes in skill set and team competency to suddenly start playing basketball instead of baseball, the underlying discipline and skills for learning, practicing, signaling, coaching, team play, incorporating feedback, and scouting the competition still apply.

Granted, there are great ball players, such as Babe Ruth and Shoeless Joe Jackson, who are born with astounding natural physical gifts. Winning pro teams, however, emerge from the evolutionary development—often starting in little leagues—of their players and the team as a whole. Using a process of stratified stability, little league coaches help young players begin by learning to catch and hit a baseball. After these basics, they proceed to learning how a playing field is set up (and which base is third), what the positions are, and how to play as part of a team. It is perfectly useless to expect double plays when the players aren't sure which way to run or where to throw the ball.

Stages in the Complexity Advantage Evolutionary Fitness Model

As with other evolutionary models reflecting the process of punctuated equilibrium, our fitness model is divided into stages or plateaus.

The first level is unconscious self-organization. Although it is, of course, possible for business enterprises to be using conscious self-organization, most—*all* in our experience—are not conscious of their self-organizing processes. Level 1 is, therefore,unconscious self-organization—that emergent organization thattakes place whether or not we know it or want it to work as it does. This is where we start. Admitting to level 1 with all of its attendant problems is an important and sometimes very difficult first step for enterprise leaders and agents. It is similar in many ways to that most difficult of statements in the AA 12-step process: "My name is John, and I am an alcoholic." For our five-step Autonomous Agent program: Who among us is comfortable saying, "My name is Mary; I'm a leader and cannot *control all* the interactions of 'my' organization"? Denying the existence of basic self-organizing patterns explained by the new complexity sciences won't make them go away.

The next four levels of our evolutionary model provide a map for encouraging the emergence of effective people, teams, and, finally, a larger enterprise. The levels are:

Level 1: recognition of unconscious self-organization

Level 2: conscious self-organization

Level 3: guided self-organization

Level 4: quantitatively guided self-organization

Level 5: consciously competent autopoiesis

Definitions of these levels can be used, first, to assess and, then, to improve enterprise performance. In going from level to level, the focus of attention moves from close personal relationships, to the more distant networking—like the ever-widening movement of ripples in a lake. First, we concentrate on building tight coupling among close colleagues on individual teams and then looser connections among teams and groups of teams in a web of interaction. This powerful web of specialized knowledge and broad experience uses disciplined process and distributed decision-making to gain stability and support change.

In striving for the complexity advantage, there is no point in rigid or surface compliance with model practices. Every business situation is different, and the environment changes continually. We adjust our *fitness to a business environment* only through functional interlocking patterns of behavior emerging from diverse agents with solid personal integrity, deep commitment, strong self-discipline, and good individual judgment.

System Characteristics in the Complexity Advantage Fitness Model

Our model draws attention to seven key enterprise system characteristics that evolve with level of fitness:

1. The first characteristic is *scale*. As we know, fitness can be measured at any one of a number of nested and intersecting system scales. Enterprise evolution begins at the individual agent or microlevel and works outward to the enterprise or macrolevel.

2. The second characteristic is the *nature of the energy providing momentum to the system*. As self-organizing systems, businesses require energy for constructing and maintaining patterns of interaction and order. The nature of this energy plays a key role in determining the space of possible agent actions and emergent behavior.

3. The third determining characteristic is found in the *context of past system learning, becoming, cognition, and change*. How

TABLE 8.1
Fitness Levels of Enterprise Self-Organization

Fitness Level	Scale to Which Attention Directed	Measurement	Enterprise Emphasis on
5 Consciously competent autopoiesis	Enterprise within its environment	Tracks patterns in enterprise and co-evolution with environment	Enterprise co-evolution in quantitatively understood internal and external environments—reflecting continuous incremental or discontinuous radical change
4 Quantitatively guided self-organization	Enterprise	Models and analysis based on statistical processes (using mean and variance data)	Enterprise using statistics and models to quantitatively understand, stabilize, and forecast trends in agent web and emergent results
3 Guided self-organization	Unit	Tracks team performance against intentions at multiple levels; links micro- and macroemergence	Committed and disciplined local teams propagating successful lessons and interlocking patterns across larger units in web within environmental context
2 Conscious self-organization	Team	Gauges team capability as performed per game plan	Committed and disciplined teams, openly communicating, learning, committing to game plans, and tracking resulting performance in environment
1 Unconscious self-organization	Agent	Yields haphazard data about unknown behavior patterns	Managers attempting to command and control agent interactions, emergent behavior, and results; self-organization seen as hidden culture

do individuals, teams, and, ultimately, the whole organization learn and adapt to their environment? What facility does the business have for developing new capabilities? What history does the enterprise have in adapting to a new landscape?

4. The *context of system alignment—micro- to macrobelonging* and *structural coupling*—is the fourth place we look for differences in maturity levels: What are the levels of commitment? How is power distributed? To what degree are agents truly autonomous?

5. In the context of *physical system being and present experience,* we look at current results of business interaction. After all, the bottom line is: What is the enterprise doing? Is it successful at this moment?

6. The sixth characteristic in the complexity advantage evolutionary model is the extent to which the enterprise is *autopoietic:* self-bounded, self-generating, and self-perpetuating. Key to strength and fitness is the extent to which a business and its people can mutually sustain one another.

7. Finally, the seventh characteristic is the holistic view of the *emergent system.* How successful is the enterprise as a whole in its selected markets? How does it act? What does it feel like?

In our model, we provide points of structure, scale, measurement, and enterprise emphasis rather than specific prescriptions. Table 8.1 summarizes key fitness levels and provides an underlying structure for further discussion in the next chapter.

The Complexity Advantage Evolutionary Fitness Model

Consciously or unconsciously, most of us accustomed to TV expect things to happen instantly. Considering our appetite for instant results, we repeat the quotation that began the last chapter: "Rome was not built in a day," and add: *Neither is a hypercycle.*

Fitness Level 1: Unconscious Self-Organization

Businesses that find themselves at level 1 are somewhat chaotic and, to some extent, mask dysfunctional cycles by surface compliance to commands and external regulation (see Table 9.1). Management focus is more on end states (*what* we have to deliver) than on how we interact to deliver it. Most people in this environment view written process as bureaucracy and, in fact, it just may be all form and no substance! It is likely that procedures aren't designed to co-evolve with the environment, quickly become obsolete, no longer add value to the job, and are—consequently—ignored. Following personal survival agendas, agents expend significant energy bumping into and stepping on each other.

TABLE 9.1
Enterprise Fitness. Level 1: Unconscious Self-Organization

View	Status	Evidence
Scale	Agent-centered microview.	Hero-driven efforts predominate.
Momentum	Competitive energy.	Fear, mistrust, and deception drive agent interactions.
Becoming	Personal learning. Joint adaptation and changes in coupling slow.	Agents hold information.
		Agents protect unique knowledge.
		Agents protect unique capabilities.
		Agents ward off change.
		Agents close own areas.
Belonging	Shallow commitments generate conflicting patterns.	Agents agree to any request.
		Agents intend best effort.
		Agents deliver as possible.
		Customer often dissatisfied.
Being	Struggling to survive in environment.	Agents make reactive personal decisions.
		Agents make self-serving trade-offs.
	Agent-to-agent interaction improvised.	Agents give lip service to joint planning, then follow personal agendas.
Autopoietic behavior and boundaries	Unconsciously, team establishes own limitations. Puts vicious cycle in place, perpetuates wasteful patterns.	Leader tries to control agent interactions by edict and demand.
		Agents pretend to follow orders.
Emergent system	Out of control coupled with victim mentality.	Agents feel victimized. Leaders feel out of control.

Explanation

Emphasis on parts not the whole system.

Competitive energy generates destructive behavior, which causes surprises and rework, thereby wasting time and money.

Information is regarded as source of power.

Agents covet subjective understanding; afraid or just not willing to share.

Agents keep lessons learned private, which makes their experience unique and them more irreplaceable.

Agents see innovation as more work and more risk.

More interested in survival of self (part) than whole.

Don't know what is doable.

Often decide what customer "really" needs.

Conflicted agent priorities and perspectives cause mixed signals and communication breakdowns.

Strained relationships at all levels of enterprise.

Agents are self-protective in reactions to environment.

Agents make invisible choices, with highest self-payback and win/lose consequences.

Agent mutual trust, respect, discipline, and consistency are lacking. Agent actions are inconsistent with game plan.

Self-organization conflicts with leader role as manager responsible for directing and controlling activity of and connection between agents. Limits power available through the whole.

Agents hide behind compliance, blindly following rules. "It's not my fault if the effort doesn't work."

Leaders command and control with increasing intensity and futility. Agents retreat to own corner, allowing others to call shots. "Tell me what to do and I'll do it. Just give me a checklist to follow."

At level 1, management tries desperately to control agent actions, interactions, and results. Agent self-organization is likely to reflect a competitive tension between authoritarian control and individual autonomy. Deception and blocked communications are indicative of defensive agent behavior. Agents regard adherence to obsolete plans or procedures and associated commitments as a game. The invisible structure emerging from self-organization in this context may be at odds with enterprise intentions. The resulting environment is characterized by uncertainty, frustration, and surprise. The first paradox that must be addressed is that of autonomy and control.

We have chosen to use personal stories for illustration here and in several other places for several reasons. First, the sharp division between work and personal life reflects an artificial and unrealistic boundary arising from an outdated paradigm that focused on the separateness of the parts rather than on their interconnections. Most of us spend a good deal more than half of our waking hours at work. We are more effective and happier when our work and personal lives are robustly integrated. Second, because the idea of self-organization is a new one for business, in many cases, there are not yet good business case studies that reflect important concepts. And, third, we have found that these stories—because they are common sense—assist those new to complexity science in beginning to identify these concepts in their everyday lives.

We are all autonomous agents, self-organizing and co-evolving with our environment. Yet our society is grounded in Newtonian thinking. Everyone's objective is to be in control. Starting at a very early age, we struggle with this paradox. Susanne provides two examples from her personal life.

One evening, when my daughter, Megan, was three, she came home from nursery school very upset:

"Mommy, can Annie command me? Annie says she can, and she commanded me to walk behind her in the lunch line." Annie was four.

"Did you do it?" I asked.

"Yes," said Megan, hanging her head.

"Then she can command you," I said, "because you let her." We talked about the need, in some cases, for authority; the need in all cases to take charge of ourselves; and our options and consequences.

My younger daughter Tara, at three, hit the control issue from the opposite angle. "Mommy," she said one day, "I want you to make me a baby sister or brother."

"Why?" I asked.

"So I can have somebody to control," Tara replied. "Everybody else around here has somebody to control." (I suggested she might try controlling the dog but got no buy-in.)

We discussed Tara's feelings about being the lowest one on the family totem pole, and I promptly forgot about the conversation. Shortly thereafter, Tara's behavior seemed a bit compulsive—she began eating only certain foods and wearing only certain clothes. I did what any parent would do: panicked and dialed the pediatrician.

He recommended letting the behavior run its course. In important areas, Tara needed to know I was the authority and would make certain decisions for her safety and well-being. In other ways, Tara needed to feel in control of herself.

For days Tara ate peanut butter and jelly, then there were weeks of spaghetti. If the target food wasn't there, she ate nothing. For two months that summer, Tara would only wear the yellow dress with red and blue ice cream cones on it. Put something else on her and moments later she was naked. She was becoming an autonomous agent and simultaneously learning that she didn't need to have someone else to "control." The person she could control was herself and in doing so, she could influence the actions of others. As convenient, we washed her ice cream cone dress at night and prepared a food of choice at meals.

At 18 Tara is a very responsible young adult and very comfortable with her autonomy. She has given up the ice cream cone dress for jeans and J Crew sweaters. Fashionable in her own style, she is not prone to quirky fads that enable teenagers (and others) to make statements of independence while gaining acceptance in their community of choice. In the course of fighting for autonomy, we see many teenagers adopt extreme styles—pierced tongues, blue hair, skirts on guys, girls with shaved heads, the abuse of drugs and alcohol, and anorexia. In their actions, they are saying: "It's *my* body; I can control it. I'll live by my own rules."

What absurdities do we generate under the tension of autonomy and control not only in our families but also in our enterprises? In a level 1 enterprise built on command and control, look around for absurd behavior. What do we do when others don't follow our rules? How are we behaving when we feel out of control, dominated, or at the end of the pecking order? What do we do when we think rules set for us are absurd?

Inside the Level 1 Organization:
The Dilbert Phenomenon

Dilbert became one of the fastest growing newspaper comic strips in the world when Scott Adams started to focus on the malaise prevalent in corporate life. On the Dilbert Web site, Adams reports that he receives "hundreds of ideas each day" from people around the world "eager to share their stories of absurd work situations and unbelievable bosses."[1]

Research studies indicate that between 65 and 80 percent of those employed are unhappy and frustrated in their work. How did literally millions of intelligent, hard-working people come to find themselves spending the better part of their lives in situations that they actively dislike but feel powerless to change? Not only is the level 1 organization ineffective, it's often unsatisfying and absurd.

In a level 1 enterprise environment, unaware of self-organization and our 14 steps, diverse agents independently self-organize and improvise on the fly to survive. The environment is full of uncertainty. We see increasing costs, long cycle times, high defects, extensive rework, staffing issues, and chaotic reaction to change. There is no focus on an interactive system at this level, and units rely on individual heroics. Activities are executed based on personal knowledge and privately held past experience. Process options are handled as hidden trade-offs and reactive decisions.

There is little team understanding of capabilities; therefore, teams make, or are coerced, into shallow commitments. The probability of meeting estimated targets is low and customers become cynical.

To move to level 2, the single most important step is to recognize and acknowledge level 1 realities.

Moving to Level 2

To move from level 1 to level 2, we need to throw out an exclusively Newtonian mind-set, add concepts from complexity sciences, and allow agents time for self-discovery. As leaders, we must relinquish our reliance on techniques of dominance and control, tear down useless bureaucracy, and focus on establishing a few key policies. A leader's job is growing an environment ripe for visible self-organization, open communication, and personal discipline among agents. Agents learn to assess their own performance accurately, understand their capabilities, and negotiate real commitments based on what's doable.

To attain level 2, everyone's focus is on complexity advantage steps 1 through 8—turning these ideas into habits. A new enterprise culture emerges from these new habits. We can tell it is a habit when people say "that's just the way we do things around here." Habits are behavior patterns supported by amplifying feedback loops. Leaders can influence amplifying loops by aligning policies, goals, visible values, and rewards behind functional patterns. Training is often required to initiate new loops. It must be followed by open agent-leader dialogue, appropriate measurement, and self-regulation.

Whether 4 or 44, there is no difference in the way we acquire habits. Recall how you got into the habit of brushing your teeth. Most likely you saw your parents or older siblings brushing their teeth (role models) and felt that it was a special, grown-up thing to do. In addition, one of your parents provided you with the toothbrush and toothpaste (tools); showed you how it was done (training); and then instructed you to "brush after every meal" (setting a policy).

But it didn't stop there. In fact, there was probably a ritual after every meal, with parents asking: "Did you brush your teeth?" "Did you brush your teeth?" "Did you brush your teeth?" This query verified that the policy was being followed—then, finally, you remembered to ask yourself: "Did I brush my teeth?" Positive reports might have been measured, and each report rewarded with a gold star on the refrigerator chart (visible evolution).

Enterprise consciousness, memory, language, habit—memes—can endure long after the people who originally helped shape them are gone. Unified enterprise behavior depends on turning a few simple rules into habits—autocatalytic loops generating stable, healthy memes for robust self-organization.

Fitness Level 2: Conscious Self-Organization

At level 2, teams of close colleagues engage in open communication and disciplined interaction (see Table 9.2). Agents consciously share knowl-

TABLE 9.2
Enterprise Fitness. Level 2: Conscious Self-Organization

View	Status	Evidence
Scale	Team centered.	Establishing basic one-to-one relationships.
Momentum	Gaining synergy; becoming more collaborative.	Direct attack on fear, mistrust, and deception.
Becoming	Team learning and adaptation obvious to outsider and exhilarating to team.	Agents share information with team.
		Team-shared knowledge.
		Common team experience.
		Agents support changes seen as beneficial to team.
		Agents protect team.
Belonging	Reliable commitments. Interlocking team patterns begin to emerge from real agent promises.	Agents negotiate deliveries.
		Agents intend to keep word.
		Agents renegotiate early when unable to keep word.
		Fewer last-minute surprises emerge.
Being	Trying to keep in step with needs of environment.	Agents participate in responsive team decisions.
		Agents participate in visible team trade-offs.
	Agent-to-agent interaction disciplined.	Agents participate in realistic team planning and follow scripts.
Autopoietic behavior and boundaries	Consciously dismantling vicious cycles.	Leader helps to surface underlying patterns (those limiting and enabling).
		Agents keep patterns visible.
Emergent system	Agents empowered. Leader focuses on setting functional environment.	Team empowers itself.

Explanation

Emphasis on team as a system: understand real power lies in relationship to others and begin to build sound relationships.

Safety nets being established for honesty and open communication; basic values of trust and respect encouraged.

Agents contribute to team power.

Qualitative understanding explicitly distributed to local agents.

Common lessons and awareness of capability informally shared.

Agents see innovation as making team more competitive and likely to survive.

Agent-enterprise alignment being built bottom up.

Agree to what all believe is doable.

Understand meaning of making a personal promise.

Fewer communication breakdowns.

More credibility in one-on-one relationships.

Agents respond to the environment using collective intellect and joint behavior.

Agents make visible, consensus-based choices, considering shared impact across collective group.

Agent activities and interactions are both planned and tracked. Bound by peer trust and respect, actions are consistent with game plan and easy to observe and measure.

Leader role is team coach, responsible for establishing commitment, discipline, and open communication among agents.

Agents encouraged to highlight sources of success and failure without repercussion.

More positive lessons learned, more ownership taken.

edge, internal game plans, and experience with teammates. The team knows the actual processes—end to end—that it uses to achieve its goals. Results of activities and interactions are measured, discussed, and jointly assessed. If we don't know how we are doing, we'll never know what behaviors to repeat (or eliminate). The objective in reaching level 2 is to make visible the way things actually work or don't work so that problems and bottlenecks are on the table and we can learn from our successes and failures. The group understands what it is doing well and the factors critical to repeating this success. Trade-offs, options, strategies for improvement, and new possibilities are discussed openly and lead to group decisions. Team patterns, structure, integrity, commitment, and learning become visible.

Hurdles and Obstacles

One of the major problems we face in moving to level 2 is the attitude we have acquired about plans and planning. This is a list of erroneous beliefs many of us hold:

1. A good plan doesn't change. If the plan changes, it was a bad plan and we have failed.

2. We must know and freeze all desired end states or final outcomes for a project before planning it.

3. Rework is bad; therefore, we should not include it in our planning. Not planning for rework will preclude it from happening.

4. Hedging our bets by doubling and tripling our estimates keeps us out of trouble by giving us more realistic time frames for completion.

5. Allowing agents or leaders to itemize risks in plans encourages them to cop out. We pay employees a lot of money to deal with the unknown.

When working with people on plans, we can tell a lot about the planning process by looking at the plans they are accustomed to preparing. What we normally find is a single-path plan that itemizes project steps for:

1. Specifying some desired outcome, product, or end state
2. Designing in detail
3. Development against the design
4. Testing the result
5. Delivering it to the customer for use

Our experience, as well as the experience of many groups we've worked with, leads us to believe that this nice neat pattern of single-path planning may be wishful thinking. Because today's environment changes so quickly, it's often hard for people at the beginning of projects to know exactly what the end state will need to look like when they reach it. And, even if they are able to provide full specifications at the start of a project, what they think they want at the beginning often changes. More realistically, projects unfold as follows:

1. Specifying some desired outcome, product, or end state
2. Designing it
3. Realizing some specifications are unclear, in conflict, or outdated due to some recent change in events
4. Reworking the specifications
5. Reworking the design
6. Developing against the design
7. Realizing some of the design is unclear, in conflict, or outdated due to some recent change in events
8. Reworking the design . . . etc.

You get the picture. There are unknowns and changing events.

Acknowledging reality often leads to a very productive discussion of the difficulties of preparing a plan that might take this version of reality into account. Because we label rework as bad, it is difficult to make plans that feature it visibly. And because we haven't tracked our actions in the past, it's hard to predict how much rework or how many iterative cycles will be likely to complete an assignment in the future. By denying the existence of rework, we are unable to uncover its contributing factors. This prevents us from becoming more efficient in the future.

If we plan only for a single iteration of a task, we reflect the need for those people doing this task only at one point in our project. It is more likely that most participants in a project will be needed at multiple points throughout. If we don't acknowledge the need for these resources, they are assigned to something else. Both projects are then disrupted by our unplanned demands on their time. If we plan to iterate tasks throughout the project, we are more likely to have the right resources available.

In the single-path plan, what happens when we track actual results? If we've marked some task as *done,* we can no longer book time against it. Assuming we don't have rework in the plan, we can't track what we are really doing. Because we're supposed to be doing some other task of our project, it's easiest to log additional time against what we're doing. Our metrics will never reflect our true performance or use of time. Without a clear understanding of our history and capabilities, we'll never become more accurate in predicting where we'll need to spend our time or how long subsequent jobs will take. If, in planning, we use our experience to include rework where it will likely occur, we can track what is actually needed against our forecast. We learn whether we need to include more or less time for the impact of change in the future.

Some leaders protest that they are accurate in their planning because they double or triple their estimates to compensate for rework and other unknowns. Although this might put the predicted time frames in range, it doesn't provide the information to improve those time frames. Only by accurately tracking where effort is expended—and wasted—can we learn to forecast and expend our effort more wisely next time around.

Visible, disciplined, yet flexible planning is a key requirement for the transition to level 2. An organization at level 2 is characterized by awakening. We write down and commit to our intended actions and interactions. Then, the entire team understands, follows, and tracks the results of the game plan. We identify options and make decisions about changes through genuine dialogue, weighing explicit alternatives and agreeing on trade-offs.

Another hurdle along the way to attaining level 2 is creating an environment in which honesty, integrity, deep commitment, and discipline are "just the way we do things around here." It is challenging to make the time required for genuine organizational learning and self-discovery. Whether or not we like the actual processes we use, there are real reasons we do what we do. We need to discover what those reasons are. Wishing things were not as they actually are won't make them so.

Those who think they don't or can't contribute to the unit's self-organization and who, therefore, don't acknowledge the need for change in their own personal behaviors are obstacles. Managers who think they have all the answers are often the very ones who know least about their organizations and the self-organization to which they contribute.

Moving to Level 3

To reach level 3, agents become more adept at observing and working with the results of team self-organization—analyzing emergent behaviors, propagating what works, and building on success. To get to level 3, we take time to learn from others. Maybe there are people in the department who excel at estimating time needed to do a job. What can we learn from them? Perhaps the whole team shares the same bottleneck of communicating with customers about their needs and conditions of satisfaction. Perhaps we can find a team in another department that used to have a similar bottleneck but has developed a solution and will share insights with us.

Agents extend team power through networking: linking similarly disciplined (level 2) teams together and rapidly spreading common memes based on the four simple rules. In fractal terms, macrounit patterns will reflect microteam patterns. More effective interlocking enterprise patterns emerge with self-similar memes in place creating a visible web of local process that evolves and supports agent interaction in a changing environment.

In working toward level 3, agents focus on complexity advantage steps 9 (doing business on the basis of synergy and collaboration) and 10 (generating social capital). To facilitate the growth of social capital, leaders focus on structures and processes that enable agents to commit visibly and effectively to others. The resulting social capital is essential for mixing and matching agent resources in response to changes in the environment. In personal computer terms, we call it *plug and play*.

Fitness Level 3: Guided Self-Organization

At level 3, agents build on the foundation established at level 2 (see Table 9.3). Now the team not only knows its processes but has turned the most effective processes into local standards replacing ineffective habits. The objective in reaching level 3 is to create a robust set of local standards that enable the unit to be effective. In addition, we generate the ability to assess new situations, understanding when new skills and resources are needed, and methods of customizing solutions to the environmental context.

Once at level 3, local teams have also loosely coupled to form larger webs of constructive unit behavior. Amplifying feedback loops and collaborative energy fuel integrated learning, commitment, and execution across teams. Leaders now have a forum for involving agents in participatory strategies and critical thinking. With common memes and coupled teams, new possibilities emerge for tighter coordination, faster cycle time to market, and lower unit costs. At level 3, agents build on group knowledge and experience to meet the enterprise goals and vision while retaining local speed and flexibility. We have the benefit of objective trade-offs and rule-based decisions for evaluating our options.

Hurdles and Obstacles

Impatience is a big obstacle to attaining level 3. It is hard not to look for shortcuts. It's even harder to accept deep in our guts that we're never finished redefining ourselves. We struggle up to level 2 learning good habits, then work really hard to establish local standards at level 3. "Whew," we say, rolling our sleeves back down, "we're finished. We have a good agreed-upon process in place; everybody's using it; and celebrations are in order." But the moment is short. Effective teams are never finished defining their proper work approach, because they're evolving and require an *evolving* work approach. If our defined approach does not evolve, interacting agents doing the work will discover better ways and—guess what?—on-the-fly improvisation and invisible self-organization begin all over again.

Another big problem at this level arises from becoming too fixed or requiring that the group function in a textbook fashion. Each team will need to experiment to find the right balance between detailing their defined approach and game plans versus using agent judgment and common sense on the field.

Moving to Level 4

The focus in the move to level 4 is on our steps 11 and 12. In step 11, we urge widespread use of powerful human symbols and abstract thought: statistical thinking, nonlinear mathematics, and complexity models. At the same time, in step 12, we encourage the business to make full use of human capital by relying on the personal judgment and basic common sense of autonomous agents.

Both abstract modeling and practical thinking are applicable to intersecting decisions at micro- and macrolevels. Patterns at one level give rise to questions or prompt desirable patterns at the next (or, a higher-level pattern prompts questions about the interaction of nested parts).

One of the biggest challenges is figuring what information to attend to and what to model, as well as what to measure and *how* to measure it. At one point in Susanne's career, she was teaching programming at AT&T. She tells this story about measurement.

One of my students (a union steward) queried whether he would be paid overtime for doing a class assignment at home. I explained that the assignment was not required but would be useful to gain the grounding needed. What ensued was a discussion of merit jobs and whether the responsibility for his proficiency lay with the company or with him. Then the question of measurement arose. The challenger persisted in the idea that it was impossible to measure thinking. And, because programming was mainly thinking, it was clearly impossible to properly measure programming efforts. How could anyone know whether he was thinking about programming while sitting in his seat? Maybe, instead, he was spending most of his day thinking about baseball. More lines of code might actually indicate lower-quality code.

Several thoughts emerged as I was against the wall. Do our measurements and rewards work against an investment in critical thought? Who do we cheat when we don't invest in learning and new or better ways of doing things? How can we encourage people to think?

TABLE 9.3
Enterprise Fitness. Level 3: Guided Self-Organization

View	Status	Evidence
Scale	Unit centered.	Team-to-team relationships being strengthened.
Momentum	Energy shared is increasing as well as constructive.	Mutual respect, trust, and honesty drive agent interactions in unit.
Becoming	Learning and evolution accelerated.	Agents in unit openly share qualitative information.
		Agent knowledge based on unit history.
		Unit experience captured.
		Agents in unit contribute to tactical innovation.
		Agents protect unit.
Belonging	Doable promises give rise to web of stable unit patterns.	Agents negotiate deliveries.
		Agents able to keep word.
		Renegotiation less frequent.
		Customer gets deliveries as expected.
Being	Current with environmental need. Well positioned for potential change. Agent-to-agent interaction defined.	Agents make unit rules and rule-based decisions.
		Agents make objective unit trade-offs.
		Agents select plays, tailor standard game plans, and share feedback on results.
Autopoietic behavior and boundaries	Conscious of amplifying feedback to imbed habits.	Leader influences emergent unit behavior.
		Agents (self-)reinforce desirable behavior.
Emergent system	Agent active part of powerful web. Leader encourages functional behavior.	Unit empowers itself through its relationship with others.

Explanation

Appreciation for networking and dependencies grow beyond immediate teams, extending power.

Honesty and open communication established; solid values of trust and respect become pervasive as ripples extend throughout the system.

Agents contribute to end-to-end unit effectiveness.

Qualitative historical data (gathered over time) explicit and sharing extended to unit colleagues.

Common lessons, performance, and capability formally shared with local agents.

Agents participate in innovative problem-solving, making themselves and the unit more valuable.

Agent alignment with enterprise continues to build.

Easier to reach agreement on what is doable.

Have more data for making a personal promise.

Less communication blockage.

Credibility between customers and suppliers enhanced.

Agents respond to environment using a few common rules derived from their own qualitative history and local success.

Agents make visible, objective choices, considering collective impacts and focusing on enterprise preservation.

Agent actions are consistent with standard set of options derived from local history and previous success, as well as easy to observe and measure.

Leader is facilitator, responsible for involving agents in participatory strategies and critical thinking.

Agent valued for contributions to new patterns.

More alliances create better data, faster learning, clearer picture, and better decisions.

It is, indeed, easier to measure the results of doing rather than thinking. Frequently, we attend to *doing* rather than *thinking* because of the physical artifacts: stacks of paper or widgets. We need new measures and models for knowledge workers in the Information Age. One of the many reasons we want deep, shared commitment and trust on the part of autonomous agents is so that we don't worry about recording and measuring individual thoughts and thinking but can, instead, measure the results of common sense and enterprise wisdom: Is the whole successful?

When writing this book, we used the number of pages produced as one of our measures, and it was a useful tool. But it would have been ludicrous to use this as our only measurement; equally important were the inspirations—just the right story, the "ah ha's," the diagrams, and that hard-to-find way of explaining an idea so it finally makes sense to others.

Fitness Level 4: Quantitatively Guided Self-Organization

At level 4, agents have an appreciation for the enterprise as an evolving "whole" and, so, develop methods for examining and simulating alternate possibilities for this dynamic system (see Table 9.4). Using mathematics, the natural language of complex adaptive systems, we articulate potential emerging scenarios for enterprise behavior self-organization and co-evolution. Teams are effectively using a wealth of quantitative tools to track and guide interaction. A quantitative history is maintained for insight into the local unit, its environment, similar entities, partners and competitors, as well as effects of the customer market and the industry.

We use models and statistical probabilities to discuss and understand our range of opportunities and the likely emergent results. Our internal and external nested and interlocking patterns are described both quantitatively and qualitatively—suggesting more stable and efficient options to achieve low cost, low waste, or quick cycle time in specific environments. Because we have mathematically supported knowledge and data-based experience, we can respond more appropriately to inevitable changes.

At level 4, leaders shift their focus to enabling agents to lead themselves. The enterprise can reap significant benefits from self-disciplined autonomous agents using internally generated rather than externally imposed regulation. It's just plain faster and more effective. This assumes, however, that agents share a clear and common vision or intent and flexible boundaries essential to business identity and auto-poietic behavior.

Hurdles and Obstacles

As we've discussed earlier, there are those who just don't believe that numbers or models can be useful in predicting people's actions and group behavior.

Another hurdle is the cost of the tools, the new eco-technicians, and the training of the entire enterprise. Many businesses will find some of the tools and expertise already resident if they look. Willingness to make the remaining investment is a matter of deep commitment.

Finally, making the boundary between a unit and its environment more permeable will be difficult for some. In our experience, leaders who prefer to go it alone and are uncomfortable with partnerships, really struggle with this one.

And this brings us to level 5: What does it take to become a consciously competent autopoietic enterprise?

Moving to Level 5

To reach level 5, we are required to achieve and sustain an autopoietic enterprise. Complexity advantage steps 13 (innovation and intellectual capital) and 14 (conscious autopoiesis) come into full force. A self-bounded, self-reflective, and self-organizing *business* will emerge from a web of agents who have lived, learned, and evolved for several years in a business environment based on the four simple rules. It takes time to apply our 14 steps—focusing on groups of steps in the stages we have just described. Here's a quick reminder:

- *At level 1, we start by recognizing and admitting where we are.*
- *To reach level 2, we focus on steps 1 through 8.*

TABLE 9.4
Enterprise Fitness. Level 4: Quantitatively Guided Co-evolution

View	Status	Evidence
Scale	Enterprisewide macroview.	Agents identify with enterprise; understand how their parts fit with whole.
Momentum	More and more constructive energy being exchanged.	Mixed messages eliminated, generating a new level of honesty and openness.
Becoming	Quantitative learning is basis of acceleration in evolution.	Agents openly share quantitative enterprise data.
		Enterprise knowledge quantitatively expressed (models and simulations).
		Agent enterprise experience quantitatively expressed.
		Agents contribute to strategic enterprise innovation.
		Agents protect enterprise.
Belonging	More effective patterns emerge with meaningful and doable promises.	All involved parties negotiate requests.
		Group's word is valuable.
		Collaboration overall high.
		Customer needs satisfied.
Being	Current with environmental need and driving new changes.	Agents make decisions based on data and modeling.
		Agents anticipate enterprise trade-offs.
		Agent-to-enterprise interactions are more stable.
Autopoietic behavior and boundaries	Developing quantitative models and simulations to enhance patterns.	Leaders forecast emergent enterprise behavior.
		Agents redirect emergent behavior that is undesirable.
Emergent system	Agents and leaders using statistical probabilities to act more effectively.	Enterprise empowers itself through mathematical representation of relationships.

Explanation

Appreciation for networking and dependencies continue to grow, completing internal web of enterprise power.

Communication opened even further. Agents begin to discuss emotions, new depth to honesty. Basis for double-loop learning being established.

Agents contribute to models and simulations, increasing enterprise effectiveness.

Quantitative and qualitative historical data (gathered over time) modeled and shared across enterprise.

Quantified lessons, expressed in models, shared throughout enterprise.

Agents participate in setting new directions for obvious niches surfaced by observations and quantitative models.

Agents are aligned with enterprise.

Agree to what all believe is "needed" and doable.

Personal respect supports strong relationships.

Supplier responsive to customer changing needs.

True customer-supplier partnership.

Agents respond to the environment guided by data derived from quantitative measures of previous success in their environment.

Agents anticipate and model statistically based choices considering enterprise options and probabilities.

Agent actions, stabilized through local history and success, are qualitatively and quantitatively monitored for trends and exceptions.

Leaders are mentors responsible for generating ability for agents to lead themselves.

Agents valued for increasing competence, thinking, and judgment.

More quantitative data and statistical modeling mean even clearer picture and better decisions supporting whole enterprise and its parts.

- *To reach level 3, we focus on complexity advantage steps 9 and 10.*
- *To reach level 4, we work on steps 11 and 12.*
- *To reach level 5, we attend primarily to complexity advantage steps 13 and 14.*

With the active participation of autonomous agents, visible interlocking patterns are continually improving—lowering unit costs, shortening cycle times, and producing products and services with little waste. Yet this desirable state of affairs—driven by amplifying feedback loops—may become too fixed.

Although effective at a particular point in a fitness landscape, we know that the landscape itself will change frequently. To move to level 5, we need to anticipate or precipitate avalanches—preferably avalanches to which our enterprise can adapt successfully. Avalanches of rapid change will occur in any case, whether or not we consciously trigger them or are prepared for them.

Now, leaders at all levels must ensure that business sensors are attuned to environmental signals to drive adaptation ahead of risk and competition. Teams and enterprise units learn how to climb fitness peaks rapidly by accelerating organizational learning. By spotting and either avoiding or building on trends and patterns, they are able to work over, around, or through avalanches as they occur. Level 5 units also cause avalanches by finding new innovative approaches to work in the business.

Using all the senses of all our agents, group intuition, models, and tools, we constantly scan the environment to bring forth information. The trick here is to trigger agents and teams into reorganizing in ways that help to sustain the enterprise whole.

Fitness Level 5: Consciously Competent Autopoiesis

At level 5, we actively work toward improving development at all levels in the business (see Table 9.5). In addition, the business and its nested teams have developed the capacity to spot and build on, or adjust for, emerging trends, thereby increasing their competitive fitness. Recognizing that no organization is completely fit for long, we have developed a web of enterprisewide mindful behavior. Intelligent adapting agents have achieved autopoietic self-organization for enterprise co-evolution with the environment. Coupled agent activities are individually and collectively executed. Experiential knowledge is applied to new product and service formulations, which are continuously updated and dynamically modeled. In this learning organization, decisions are based on values and competitive enterprise trade-offs. The emergent environment is highly innovative.

Hurdles and Obstacles

A major hurdle on the way to level 5 is self-satisfaction. Teams and business should be very proud of the work they've done to get to level 4. Because we've been working on disciplined and visible processes in the climb through four levels—which generally takes 5 to 10 years—we are likely to find that the continuing push in these areas creates a major pitfall on the way to level 5: We've become too rigid. Our rigidity can literally make us blind and unable to see new trends, whether internal or external.

Moving from Level to Level of the Complexity Advantage Evolutionary Fitness Model

We devoted a much larger portion of the material in this chapter to levels 1 and 2 and the transition from level 1 to level 2 than to any other transition. This is because the first transition is the most difficult.

In Chapter 6, we stressed the importance of getting the basic person-to-person relationships working effectively so that they can form building blocks for the enterprise. For the moment, we want to say the same thing in a converse statement: If something *isn't* working, give the fundamental parts as much time and attention as they need to establish

TABLE 9.5
Enterprise Fitness. Level 5: Consciously Competent Autopoiesis

View	Status	Evidence
Scale	Enterprise within environment, a macroview plus.	Agents identify with enterprise and understand how they help the whole fit with the environment.
Momentum	Strong collaborative energy exchanged.	Double-loop learning in place.
Becoming	Speed of agent joint learning drives enterprise evolution ahead of others.	Agents openly share with enterprise partners.
		Agents create intellectual capital for enterprise.
		Agents forecast probabilities and trends of future enterprise experience.
		Agents see part of their job as enterprise innovation.
		Agents protect enterprise ecology.
Belonging	Supported by deep commitment.	Agents brainstorm requests.
		Agents value ideas and commitments.
		Agents negotiate new ideas.
		Stakeholder needs satisfied.
Being	At the edge, far from equilibrium.	Agents make value-based enterprise decisions.
		Agents make trade-offs for enterprise success.
		Stable but evolving agent-to-enterprise interactions.
Autopoietic behavior and boundaries	Consciously aligning patterns to emergent environment.	Leaders forecast emergent enterprise and environment.
		Agents help to reinforce or redirect needed patterns.
Emergent system	Powerful agents generating co-evolving web.	Enterprise empowers itself through thinking, autonomous agents.

Explanation

Appreciation for networking and dependencies continue to grow, extending web to a virtual enterprise, including external partnerships with customers and other suppliers.

High level of constructive energy fueled by quality of knowledge, experience, and wisdom shared.

Agents learn faster through win-win relationships.

Agents encouraged to think, use judgment, and develop new ideas and concepts.

Cumulative agent experience and projections guide enterprise direction.

Virtual research and development throughout the enterprise perceived to be part of all agent jobs.

Agents are aligned with enterprise and needs it serves.

Jointly discover and ascertain what is needed and what is doable.

Joint commitment to relationship behind success.

Supplier anticipates customer changing needs.

Customer delighted, generating deep and committed loyalty.

Agents respond to the environment using value-based thinking via cost-benefit data, analyzed and modeled over time across enterprise.

Agents anticipate and model statistically based choices considering enterprise capabilities and possibilities for competitive success.

Agent actions qualitatively and quantitatively monitored for trends or exceptions, and analyzed or modeled for new possibilities.

Leaders drive adaptation ahead of competition and risk. When necessary, create chaos to ward off growing stability.

Agent valued for pattern creation.

Clearer picture to all in enterprise encourages more options, alternatives, and possibilities to surface—leading to more effective co-evolution.

TABLE 9.6
Fitness Levels of Enterprise Self-Organization

Fitness Level	Process	Decisions	Trade-offs	Knowledge	Experience
5 Consciously competent autopoiesis	Enterprise always improving	Value-based	Mutually beneficial	Phylogeny and overlapped ontogeny	Dynamic and changing
4 Quantitatively guided self-organization	Based on group statistics	Data-based	Anticipated	History-, model-, and simulation-based	Quantified
3 Guided self-organization	Unit options that work	Rule-based	Objective	History- and team-based	Leveraged
2 Conscious self-organization	Loyal to team plan	Interactive	Visible	Team-based	Common and public
1 Unconscious self-organization	Agent ad hoc	Reactive	Unclear	Personal	Private

their own autonomy and effective interaction. However frustrating and slow evolution seems, building on unsound fundamentals is more costly in the long run.

Summary: Points of Focus for the Complexity Advantage Fitness Levels

The complexity advantage evolutionary fitness model summarizes a series of very significant changes in our basic approach to business. In closing this chapter, we want to return to the starting point: Rome wasn't built in a day. Following a pattern of punctuated equilibrium, we should expect that in the most effective of enterprises, the evolution from level 1 to level 5 will take years—Six Sigma at Motorola took 14 years. Although most of the transition work is at the agent level and in the trenches, a summary roadmap may provide both an overview of the whole process as well as key indicators for each level. Table 9.6 summarizes the characteristics of each fitness level in five key areas:

1. The nature of processes taking place within the enterprise
2. The ways in which decisions are made
3. The types of trade-offs taken into account during decision making
4. The attributes of enterprise knowledge
5. The types of agent experience available to the enterprise

Working in a Living System

Chapter Ten

Autonomous Agents

I n his book about Harry S. Truman,[1] Alfred Steinberg described a sign Truman kept on his desk while he was President of the United States (1945–1950). It said: "The buck stops here."

To which we say: *autre temps, autre mœurs* (other times, other ways). Now *every* desk should have a sign that says: "The buck stops here." No matter what role he or she assumes in a business, every person is first and foremost an autonomous agent.

In a highly competitive global market, businesses need all agents to keep an eye on the future, providing projections of the ways in which their domains are evolving. As specialists close to our own performance, capability, trends, and changing customer needs, we continually generate a selection of potential and probable scenarios. Leader and synergistic agents aggregate these scenarios and feed back common and newly emerging enterprise patterns, intentions, and opportunities. *Voilà*, enterprise unity emerges—enabling product and service delivery to evolve with, or ideally just ahead of, the market.

In this chapter we discuss agents who wish to function effectively in the business enterprise. In a nutshell, we as agents (1) begin by focusing our attention on the four simple rules—strengthening our effective habits and changing our behavior where necessary. Simultaneously, agents (2) follow an individual plan for learning about and testing the "new" complexity science as a mechanism that generates useful explanations. With these well under way, we can then (3) use the sequence described in the complexity advantage evolutionary fitness model to embark on mastering the 14 steps for success. We should work on the steps individually as well as with the members of our work groups. Finally, with as much empathy, self-awareness, and style as we can muster, as leader agents (this need not be related to a hierarchical position in any way), we should (4) both lead by example and assist in generating an open, collaborative environment in which others can also contribute effectively. In this chapter, we attend primarily to the application of the four simple rules.

Although the prescriptions in this chapter bear some resemblance to various sets of ethical and religious rules promulgated elsewhere, they are derived from the application of complexity science to our business experience. We do not offer them because they will engender goodness (although we're not unhappy if this is a by-product). We suggest that our readers engage their autonomy by testing these ideas for effectiveness in their businesses, bearing in mind that these types of changes take a long time to show results.

Businesses Need Agents Who Are Willing to Be Respectful, Honest, and Trusting

To be effective within an organization, we must be willing and able to perform our individual responsibilities. However, what we do individually makes up only a small percentage of our contribution to the enterprise. We must also be willing to coexist in an environment of mutual respect. This requires that we replace an artificially generated "respect" based solely on authority, power, or dominance with a more difficult respect. This new respect is one grounded in the recognition that every person has the right, the responsibility, and is actually constructed by nature to organize a personal version of a reality. Reality is neither totally objective nor totally subjective, but consensual. Our sense of reality emerges from our human dialogue (in language) and thinking (internalized language) to describe our environment. Each of us ħ. unique set of experiences to bring to the human sense-making proc Because the world is so complex, an effective business will make use of the larger space of possibilities generated by multiple versions of common "reality." This is not to say, by the way, that it is inappropriate to accord *additional* respect to those whose experience or sense-making we find of particular value.

To provide a concrete example of effective autonomy and personal two-way respect without regard to age, authority, or power, Susanne turns again to experiences with her daughters. Susanne's story:

When my daughters were young, they would meet me at the door when I came home from work. Sometimes, when my workday had been very stressful, coincidentally the girls would accost me with the high-decibel screeching or petty sibling spats that all children indulge in. I'd find myself saying: "Mommy's had a hard day. Please quiet down and just leave me alone for a little bit."

My daughters always respected this request. At some point in the evening, regardless of my day, I'd ask my daughters how their days had been.

One evening when I asked three-year-old Tara about her day at nursery school, she said: "I had hard day, Mommy; leave me be."

Taken aback for a moment, I paused, then responded: "I'm sorry you've had a hard day." And *let her be.* So often we automatically assume that our positions of authority give us the right to demand respect and then take it for granted. How often do we listen to, rather than ignore, the hidden plea from others to be respected in return? Our reality is no more real or more important than anyone else's. Every person's existence, feelings, perspective, and right to be respected is as legitimate as our own. Respect only works if it goes in two directions.

Leader agents play a critical role in overtly extending this two-way respect. One of the marked qualities of business executives who are highly successful is their ability to listen carefully to everyone. Particularly when someone is presenting a new idea or an idea that contradicts an established point of view, they take time to probe, ask questions, and engage in dialogue to digest new concepts.

Genuine two-way respect opens the possibility of full and open communication. For the most part, we humans don't like to put ourselves at risk, to admit mistakes, or expose vulnerabilities. But sharing vulnerabilities may be one of the most important skills we can develop to reap the full benefit of self-organization. We will be far more effective if we know and overtly deal with not only team member strengths, but also their biases, blind sides, and emotions. If we can bring ourselves to tell others what we're not good at, they can fill in for us, create a special niche where we can thrive, or even help us gain experience and expertise.

Open communication is not as easy as it might seem, even in cases where there is no abuse of power or authority. By nature we are collaborative, eager to have others be agreeable, keep conflict at a minimum, and approve of our actions. Respect may not be enough to encourage us to openly exchange diverse perspectives, generate disagreement, engage in healthy conflict, and then take responsibility for ourselves. Processes that encourage open discussion and dialogue, yet leave responsibility where it belongs, are very important. A related story from Susanne:

When my older daughter Megan was a teenager, we faced some of the genuine difficulties inherent in open communication. On a memorable occasion, Megan felt very strongly about a course of action that I didn't approve of. The conversation went around in circles until all of a sudden I was stopped cold in my tracks as Megan, in tears, said:

"Please, Mom, don't make me lie to you."

There it was; I realized that my daughter was becoming an adult and had to make her own decisions. In time, we learned to agree that we could disagree. Megan would discuss her pending choices and decisions with me in confidence. She could decide for herself *and* tell me of those choices in confidence. I could listen without comment—which did not mean that I agreed with or condoned the associated behavior. It was so hard to hear things I didn't want to hear *and* not pull rank or take action. With great difficulty I listened in confidence to Megan's stories, which included things about her friends, things that I knew their parents—my friends—would want to know. In my choice to be informed and less vulnerable to surprises, I had to accept the consequences. I had to face the reality of not being in control. I've heard parents admonish their children, "Don't ever let me catch *you* drinking!" You know, they never did catch them. Unfortunately, it did not mean they weren't doing it. I cringe every time I hear managers say, "Don't ever let me catch anyone. . . ." They won't—but neither will they control the behavior.

In some cases, I've had to pick up the pieces in situations I might have felt I could or should have tried to control. Instead of a false sense that I have everything under control, I have a more accurate assessment of what is going on and what the consequences might be. Open communication is not only about two-way personal respect; it's also replacing the illusion of control with shared rules—such as trust—and leaving others with accountability and responsibility for their own actions.

In our work as internal and external consultants, we frequently facilitate organizational self-assessment or strategic planning meetings. To deal with difficult problems that will enable a group to move to the next level of fitness, those meeting often agree that certain information exchanged in open conversation will remain in the room. Only through assuring confidentiality are we able to surface and address issues.

Who among us is willing to share information when we feel that to do so will put us at risk? Not many! It is for this reason that problems remain hidden or, in any case, unresolved.

Today's *un*discussable information is important. Managers who don't trust often hold themselves accountable for every decision in their group and frequently put pressure on agents to break promises of confidentiality. In so doing, they propagate the vicious cycle of mistrust, deception, and fear. To break out of this cycle, agents must be willing to deal with the consequences of their actions—including maintaining trust and confidence against pressure. For consulting agents, this can mean losing a client.

Respect and trust are tied together. Urgency and authority provide no excuse for breech of promise; ask any doctor, lawyer, or parish priest. Open communication brings with it a lot of information, as well as the responsibility for using that information appropriately. Here again, there are opportunities for leader agents to lead by example. In time, as trust grows, more and more agents will be comfortable sharing need-to-know information on a broader basis—the hypercycle emerges.

Businesses Need Agents Who Are Able to Understand Their Capabilities and Fitness Levels

Fitness is a measure of how well a system adapts within its context and environment. To understand their fitness levels, autonomous agents must have an accurate understanding of their individual capabilities.

We have long used ranges of measures to estimate and predict physical fitness, such as body temperature, cholesterol levels, blood pressure, and white and red blood cell counts. Homeostasis is the human body's self-regulatory mechanism that allows changes within appropriate tolerance levels. Actual performance and capacity testing is also becoming more common, in such tests as treadmill aerobic testing.

In many aspects of our lives, we can assess our performance or the history of actual results. After committing to and executing a course of action, we evaluate our measured results. Suppose Susanne commits to cycle a 12-mile course every morning (Mary Ann does karate instead). Susanne notes how long it takes her to complete the course each day. It is likely that she will ride at different speeds on different days. In this example, her performance ranges anywhere between:

- *Forty-five minutes on Monday, when she's somewhat rested from the weekend*
- *Fifty minutes on Tuesday*
- *Sixty minutes on a bad Wednesday*
- *Fifty-five minutes on Thursday*
- *Forty minutes on Friday with the wind at her back*
- *Forty-five minutes again on Saturday*

Her performance varies, but the average is somewhere around 50 minutes (see Figure 10.1).

Recording our performance—keeping a history of the results achieved by a person following a known course of actions—helps keep us

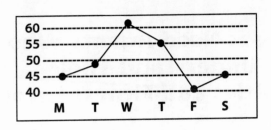

FIGURE 10.1
**Cycling Capacity: Range of 40 to 60 Minutes.
Approximate Average of 50 Minutes.**

honest about the actual results. Most of us are inclined either to over- or underremember our performance. Accurate tracking is key to personal self-awareness and the potential for change. If a course of action tends to result in visible outcomes that are positive, we are encouraged to repeat it. If the results are negative, we can consciously intervene to change or move away from that course of action in the future. And, if results are not consciously considered, we will most likely continue out of habit.

We measure our performance to understand our capabilities. Capabilities are the range of expected results that can be achieved by a person following a known course of action. In addition, a known capability is a predictor of probable future outcomes of that course of action. If we can't or don't measure our current performance, it is difficult to predict what we're capable of. Performance improvement is unlikely.

In addition, understanding one's capability is the key to making meaningful commitments. If you tend to cycle 12 miles in 40 to 60 minutes and someone suggests that you enter a race that requires a 3-minute mile, you have data on which to decide whether entry in the race would be prudent. In addition, your capability is likely to continue in its current pattern unless you undertake a focused program of behavior change. If you are capable of cycling a 5-minute mile today, you will not be able to ride a 3-minute mile tomorrow by arbitrarily committing to do so.

Businesses Need Agents Who Take Seriously Commitment to What Must Be Done

Obviously, it is critical that we, as member agents of a workplace team, commit to learning and consistency in *what's*. Due to enterprise pressures, avalanches from a complex and rapidly changing environment, and histories of our interactions, the simple act of committing has become less simple. Mary Ann's experience in writing this book provides a perfect example. It was both exhilarating and excruciating. Just ask any of her friends. In her own words:

While working on this book, I wanted to change my inclination to agree to deadlines that are too short. OK, I'll admit it, I'm an over-achiever! I've had a career pattern of acquiescing to project time frames that were not quite impossible but that were not doable with quality in the course of a "normal, aggressive" workday. (Note what the words tell you about my choice of environment.)

To start my behavior change, first I had to admit to my history of prior performances—sometimes as a tired-but-praised hero, sometimes winning the game of chicken because others failed first, sometimes missing the deadline and surprising others. Because I have been making unrealistic commitments on and off for years and because I have been consistently rewarded for doing so, this behavior pattern, this structural coupling, is very strong. Although I have become more acutely aware of my behavior by writing about it and think that I want to make this change, I find myself slipping into the old behavior pattern automatically. Because I could recognize the pattern and reflect on it, even though I have not yet changed it, I have taken an important step. This is called the *feeling guilty* stage.

Because of my emergent human capabilities (thinking and self-reflection), I have decided to change my structurally coupled habit of agreeing when I know my probable capacity in a rational workday does not match the requested timing. As I started to implement this decision, I felt very awkward. I was not practiced in this new pattern; and, when I tried to implement it, it was both difficult and embarrassing. I would occasionally blurt out my schedule estimate abruptly, giving no indication of my willingness to discuss alternatives. Then, catching myself, the next time I would state my ability to deliver so softly that no one could possibly hear it. Making this worse, when my new behavior surprised Susanne, sometimes she responded favorably and sometimes not—depending on when I caught her.

As we turn in this manuscript, I am still in this vulnerable state. Through dogged persistence and with lots of help from my family, Susanne, and other friends, I am beginning to set more realistic deadlines. The behavior change process is not yet complete. My new structural coupling is not yet very strong, and so it is easy, unfortunately, to backslide to the older entrenched habits. I expect that I will need to continue to consciously engage this new behavior for at least a year before I develop a functional habit that is triggered automatically by the request for project timing. Perhaps by the next book.

Businesses Need Agents Who Can Make Visible How Things Are Really Done

To coordinate group behavior effectively, we agents need open dialogues on the target and actual results of our actions and interactions (*what* is being done). We also need interaction concerning the ways in which we plan to accomplish and actually deliver these results (*how* we do it). If we don't know how a job is going to get done, we are unlikely to know if it is off track. And, because changes to plans almost always happen during implementation, if we don't make these changes visible, we won't have any idea how we ended up where we are.

The *how* emerges from responsible agents through an active and creative discovery of what works for us in that setting. We need to capture and share these lessons learned—devising evolving collective approaches. In some cases we may be able to adapt—but never simply adopt—other methods or textbook solutions from remote agents (products of a slightly different ontology and environment). Because each business and each team is unique, we are the only ones who *can* know how our individual teams work together.

Many of us as leaders or coordinators have experienced some visible or invisible variant of the following conversation:

"Oh, you want a plan? No problem, tell me what you want. I'll give you your plan."

"No, not *my* plan, a real, jointly constructed, usable plan to guide the work."

"Whatever, here's a plan."

Everyone knows that such a plan exists only on paper. And we know this team is going back to improvisation. What we don't know is how this complete negation of anything other than the form of creating a plan emerged as a coupled process in this team. Did the leader redo prior plans? Did the agents not want to take real responsibility for reporting the real situation? In either case, this process is worse than useless. It wastes time and energy and is likely—by the bare fact of its existence—to prevent real planning.

The target is to first make visible the team's work as it actually occurs. Then, keep that work as close to a game plan as possible so that measurement is meaningful and prescriptions based on our measurement are closely aligned with reality.

Most of us either have had the experience—or know someone who has had the experience—of being placed on a strict diet by a doctor to bring a blood pressure, cholesterol, or body weight measurement into an acceptable range. You walk away with the prescribed diet in hand and return in two months for a follow-up measurement. The question is: What will the new measurement reflect? The efficacy of the diet? The results of your eating behavior? Or both? If you followed the diet, the answer is both. If not, the new measurement provides an assessment of the results of your behavior but *not* of the diet prescribed.

Many diets have been discarded as ineffective, not because the diet didn't work but because the person "following" it improvised. "Well, I had to go to a business lunch," we might say; or, "I ran out of grapefruit and I ate something else. I don't exactly remember what, or how much. . . ." The result is a measurement, but not the information needed to correct our immediate or ongoing course of action. Because we are not sure what happened, there is no effective way of adjusting the prescription—which may, in fact, work if followed. Just so with the process of agent interaction.

The first step in visible co-evolution is that autonomous agents *think*—seriously weigh history, needs, and options. The output of our thinking is input to what we *do*. Then we *check* the results of what we have done. The output of the checking is the input to *taking action*—adjusting our game plan. The plan grows, evolves, and remains consistent with the doing, and there are fewer mysteries about how we got where we are or where we're going. We will never have full visibility of the entire context surrounding us. Our environment will always be subject to uncertainty. Nevertheless, keeping track of the order and patterns that we can see helps us to establish expected boundaries within the instability.

To generate or regenerate our own positive environment, we as agents must be willing to hold ourselves accountable for our individual contributions to visible self-organization. We need to put mirrors in place to continually reassess our own actions and interactions—both effective and ineffective. Leader agents must not only participate in this self-awareness but also provide an environment where this can occur.

We know a young girl, the daughter of friends. Measurements—or a periodic glance in her direction—showed that she was losing weight very quickly. Her eating habits were visible to her family: They dined together at least twice a day. Friends attested to healthy lunches consumed at school. Hidden and invisible behavior was the problem. It was impossible to help this bulimic child until her invisible behavior (induced vomiting) was made visible, diagnosed, and addressed directly.

Measurements and metrics are only useful when all agents are acting according to the game plan—or making their deviations visible as soon as possible. If we're loyal to a plan, we can determine which parts of our approach went well and which didn't. We can learn about our bottlenecks and pitfalls. When they're visible and we know what they are, we can work together to adjust our processes as necessary. Even with volumes of metrics, it is impossible to improve behavioral patterns that are invisible.

Autonomous Agents Within Business Enterprises

> *"Life is trouble,"* Zorba continued. *"Death, no."*
> FROM THE 1946 NOVEL, *ZORBA THE GREEK*[2]

"Just" to apply the four simple rules is a lot of work. By being unique and autonomous, we human beings create a lot of trouble for ourselves and for each other. We find it useful from time to time to remind ourselves of the rich benefits accruing to a business that is able to make full use of social, human, and intellectual capital.

Agents as Parts Within Business Enterprise Co-evolution

Even though approximately 90 percent of the cells in our bodies are replaced every seven years, body patterns and individual consciousness remain intact. A business enterprise with strong memes reflects similar autopoietic longevity. Mary Ann relates: "When I recently visited a customer service organization I had set up 15 years ago, only 7 of the original 200 people were still working there. But it felt largely the same: Many of the processes, traditions, and words used originally were still in use. The commitment to provide superb customer service was intact. Thursday was still bagel day, and team meetings continued to follow the same agenda (admittedly, with very different content)."

It is unrealistic to expect to create all new patterns of agent interaction every time an employee leaves. And neither businesses nor employees can—or want—to depend on lifetime relationships. Business sustainability depends on the strength and nature of enterprise memes and concomitant culture. Enterprise culture emerges over time from the interaction of its member agents. A hypercycle culture helps us move rapidly, is in tune with its parts, but has balancing tension. It is customized to the employees and the purpose they serve. After all, the memes of an enterprise are a direct result of patterns in recursive agent interactions.

No two people, teams, organizations, or environmental conditions are exactly alike. When configuring for high performance, there is no "one size fits all." The processes of customizing for local conditions and building in procedural flexibility to promote agent thinking are essential to the competitive character of the business. However, it is not enough to provide a functional environment.

Each hypercyclist is also individually responsible for recognizing himself or herself as part of a professional team, retaining a clear vision of the landscape the team must transverse and maintaining strong individual skills. To co-evolve successfully in the midst of changing landscapes, each team member must remain in training—working continually to increase both individual capability and team fitness.

Distributed Control

In the face of today's rapid change, some business enterprises have been erroneously moving away from the agent habits and disciplines that sustain a hypercycle culture. Under competitive pressure, they have, as examples, eliminated distributed control to reduce costs or sacrificed responsible agent thinking for standardized mindless compliance. These behaviors may indeed produce short-term momentary rewards, but, over time, the business loses its organizational plasticity. When the inevitable changes occur, there are no memes that engage agent thinking, communication links, and flexible behaviors. Unable to assess the change and instantaneously (re)organize to accommodate it, hundreds of thousands of autonomous agents might as well be robots.

To survive, an enterprise is dependent on autonomous agents who are aware of and forthright in providing appropriate information about internal and external issues, trends, and possibilities. Ultimately, if agents cannot embrace integrity, sharing, commitment, discipline, and personal mastery of change, they must be removed.

The Risks in This Brave New World

There are, of course, risks in adopting the four simple rules before the enterprise in which you work establishes a functional and supportive environment. Saying "no" when everyone else says "yes" can lead to being ostracized or removed from the team. The risks are real—although we sometimes magnify them out of proportion to reality. Because our emotional state determines our possible options, if we feel we have no choices, we, in fact, have no choices. Being fully autonomous involves making choices and incurring consequential risks.

On the other hand, we can choose to give up our claims to autonomy, spending our lives unhappy, unfulfilled, angry at "them," and conducting business on vicious cycles. While giving the illusion of safety, this may be the riskiest approach of all. According to Charles H. Mayo in *365 Meditations for People Who (May) Worry Too Much:*

Worry affects circulation, the heart and the glands, the whole nervous system, and profoundly affects the heart. I have never known a man who died from overwork, but many who died from doubt.[3]

Resiliency

It is the nature of our world to be both complex and ever changing. Because change is inherently disruptive, we—as individuals as well as businesses—will be upset, thrown for a loss by a ball out of left field or a major avalanche of new technologies, and need to reorganize from time to time. Just as in other dissipative systems, we need energy to be able to learn and grow rather than cling to rigidity or, worse, dissolve into chaos.

Resiliency is the capacity to reorganize easily and effectively in response to both small and large events. Resiliency emerges in individuals who are fully autonomous and who have a sense of wholeness or completeness within themselves. People who are complete in themselves are able to take positive actions in response to any type of change. Resiliency arises from flexibility and a willingness to engage a wide variety of potential outcomes. In many cases, resilient people adapt well to change not because they are reactive and totally freewheeling, but because they are focused and disciplined and, therefore, have a self-aware history of their reorganizational responses in the past and a homeostatic *expectation of emerging successfully from future changes.* As President John Fitzgerald Kennedy said in his inaugural address, January 10, 1961:

All this will not be finished in the first one hundred days. Nor will it be finished in the first one thousand days, nor in the life of this Administration, nor even perhaps in our lifetime on this planet. But let us begin.[4]

Chapter Eleven

Leaders

L ike learning to ski by leaning out and down the mountain or to countersteer a motorcycle by guiding it in the opposite direction from the way you want to go, changing your leadership style takes both courage and personal experience. There are some guideposts; others have done it; but the activity is personal. This chapter focuses on guideposts that help business leaders make changes in their personal approach to business, taking into account the ideas from complexity and self-organization.

Changing Leadership Fitness Landscapes

A leader's successful approach with agents in one context can easily lead to failure with another. Well before complexity science, business recognized the need to fit leadership style to context in two well-known cases:

- *First, in software development, the phenomenon called SSS (Sec-*
ond System Syndrome*). New project managers, highly successful*

in one context, are often rewarded by an opportunity to lead a larger, second, similar but slightly different effort. Here they try to repeat their success using the same techniques in a different context and meet disastrous results.

- *Second, and more generally, the Peter Principle describes middle managers who have avoided failure by remaining in the same environment. They are often fooled into believing a single approach works everywhere, until they fail miserably—resulting in the end of a career or, if lucky, a valuable lesson about context.*

Now the business landscape is changing radically everywhere. Competitive advantage no longer lies in a 2- to 20-year plan constructed by specialists. In the Information Age, most sources of competitive advantage reside in a business's capacity to tap the collective intelligence of staff members and in the ability of the business team to work together to create value for customers. One way or another, businesses are in the knowledge business. The result of an amplifying feedback loop, knowledge is currently doubling every year; and this rate will only accelerate. This means that successful firms and leaders must be able to extend knowledge and competence from one unit to another more quickly.

Most businesses are better at extending competence in place rather than transplanting it across units. Changes in management and reorganization of units are two techniques often used when attempting to leverage competencies across units. The old management paradigm assumes that the competency rests with the single agent who commands and controls the others. In fact, it rests with the interlocking behaviors of all of the agents involved and in the environment supporting those behaviors.

If enterprise memes are based on experience with and local application of the four simple rules, leaders and teams can easily mix and match for effective dialogue and fluid team efforts. They no longer have to stop first to develop a common language and establish some basis for relationships. When agents are aware of and accustomed to surfacing differences in context, new ideas, and possibilities, competencies can spread quickly and naturally (like smiles), become contagious, and emerge throughout the enterprise.

Using the concepts of complex self-organization, a business leader's goals are to:

1. Influence agent interaction and relationships in ways that satisfy employees in their natural tendency toward sense-making and collaborative behavior.

2. Encourage emergent behavior that supports enterprise sustainability, growth, and evolution.

Leadership involves generating contexts in which effective employee interaction can be realized consistently. Most critically, it entails establishing and maintaining a robust open communication and decision-making network. Timely feedback can be built in to bring enterprise and environmental patterns and trends to the surface.

Self-Organizing Leadership Techniques

As enterprise leaders, we must find tools and techniques that help bring order—not control—to patterns of dynamic connectedness. Our leadership techniques must not only support existing contexts but also provide for the creation of new ones. We must simultaneously help stabilize, yet continually transform, agent interactions and emergent patterns of group behavior. Because commanding and controlling the enterprise is largely impossible, we think that the word *manager* is outdated. We use the word *leader* instead and believe that the nature of the change in language also suggests a change in appropriate approach and responsibilities.

We would certainly *not* suggest that all previously used tools and methods be discarded, only that they be reevaluated through our new lens of complexity thinking. For those approaches that have worked well for us, we may develop new insights into why they work (such as balanced scorecards). For other tools or models that at times have been quite useful but at other times less reliable, we may be able to determine the problem areas and be able to realign them with complexity science to realize more consistency (Deming's TQM, for instance). For yet other management fads and fashions that have entered the management game with a roar and exited the field with their tails between their legs, the reason for their difficulties should become clear (for us, the problems with reengineering fall in this category). Complexity science helps us to screen for leadership approaches with a higher probability of success and to avoid flavor-of-the-month remedies.

Many leaders have effective processes in their repertoire to guide organizational change. In examining our individual techniques, we may find some need to be discarded and others need only small tweaks. Here's an example.

Engendering New Habits and Memes

Many leaders will both recognize their own behavior in these steps to develop good business habits and note some complexity tweaks:

1. Being a role model
2. Providing tools and opportunities for learning
3. Setting evolving policies
4. Verifying through a web of dialogue that policies are being followed
5. Measuring and rewarding the emergent behavior

Staffing the Business

Recruiting and keeping the agents best suited to a business is an essential leadership responsibility. The change in business environment has not only altered the traditional role of manager, it has also created the need for several new functions. An effective organization will, of course, employ only autonomous agents rather than mechanical cogs. In addition, during both the transition to and while sustaining level 5 fitness, agents may take on roles as catalysts and what we have labeled eco-technicians. Human catalysts mirror the function provided by chemical catalysts—triggering and speeding up organizational change. Highly skilled in the mathematics and models of complexity, eco-technicians monitor the business environment; the nature and strength of amplifying or balancing feedback loops; the energy and information flows in and out; and the results. Similar to ecologists and environmental engineers, eco-technicians provide the information needed in a self-organizing business to develop hypercycles and influence ecological adjustments for sustainability. Until teams can do this for themselves, leaders will be responsible for selecting and installing catalysts and eco-technicians. Later in this chapter, we describe the key characteristics for both roles.

Key Techniques

Our new leadership approaches must be grounded not in a deterministic pursuit of *right* answers but in the dynamic generation of meaningful questions. An open, questioning atmosphere is necessary to diminish fear of being wrong and to instead expand possibilities for being. To do this, a leader:

1. Personally embodies and continually communicates the strategic direction of the firm and the complexity advantage steps for success

2. Reduces the power hierarchy and ensures that vicious cycles are removed

3. Helps to assemble a powerful communication and decision-making web

4. Recruits, attracts, and retains diverse autonomous agents well suited to the nature of the firm

5. Selects and supports the catalysts and eco-technicians critical to effective organizational evolution

6. Encourages the four simple rules and their associated habits and memes through appropriate personal attention, policies, dialogue, measurement, and rewards

7. Pumps energy and information into the business

8. Practices patience

9. Strives for *good enough* emergent capabilities and performance—not an impossible and stultifying perfect fit

Reducing the Artificial, Designated Power Hierarchy and Enabling Natural Organization

There are many techniques circulating today that are aimed at generating a more facilitative leadership style, including team building, mentoring, and coaching. In addition, newer tools and models abound for mitigating the concentration or abuse of power: matrix management, 360° feedback, resource pools, as well as networked and webbed organizational structures. Many of these are useful and should, with the help of local autonomous agents, be considered for appropriateness. The degree to which these and other tools will be effective is directly related to each leader's underlying personal behavior, attitudes, and habits.

In his introduction to *Battle Ground Berlin: CIA versus KGB in the Cold War* (very unusually written by the book's editor at Yale University Press), Jonathon Brent wrote:

> It could be said that the Soviet people were betrayed by their leaders. Why? Because ideological commitments and all-consuming interest in protecting power were always paramount to those leaders—stifling their ability to see things, to use Matthew Arnold's homely phrase, "as in themselves they really are." Although they possessed often superior information and much more of it, the Soviets could not put it sufficiently to their larger advantage. They won battle after battle but lost the war. Rarely did Stalin receive information that he might not like. Rarely was the social or political reality of the West portrayed to Soviet leaders for what it was. Most often Soviet leaders would be told what they wished to hear and would see what their ideology told them they must. When Gorbachev attempted to reverse this, the system fell apart.[1]

Because much of leaders' time is spent in management reviews, the review process provides a significant opportunity for generating change. In a power hierarchy, upward communication tends to be sales presentations orchestrated for two purposes. First, subordinates often "sell" their individual fitness by trying to appear flawless and totally in control. And, second, subordinates sell the pluses and minuses involved in their decisions. By selling their decisions upward, they co-opt their "superiors" into shared ownership in the decision and, thereby, delegate at least partial responsibility or accountability up to them.

Operating decisions are better left in the hands of the responsible agents. Leaders often lack detailed understanding of the implications behind such decisions, which teams of member agents have naturally gained through experience. Agents spend substantial time and energy on sales presentations, engaging more form than content. It is amazing how much agent time is spent discussing how to sell effectively to different leaders. While it is appropriate to take into account each person's natural inclinations when engaging in a dialogue, it is not useful to invest effort in tailoring facts and actions to match "what the boss really wants to hear," distorting an agent's individual perceptions and diminishing the agent's value.

As leaders, we must remove the opportunities for wasting enterprise resources on upward selling. This means supporting appropriate agent and team decision making rather than assuming responsibility ourselves. We must take the responsibility for redirecting agent survival games—holding back cards, scoring points, or engaging the coach-leader to substitute for them in the game—that have emerged from power hierarchies.

When we replace presentations with true dialogue sessions, we are taking an important step toward accomplishing several objectives. First, and an important part of the processes necessary to reach fitness level 2, dialogue is useful for getting issues on the table and initiating problem solving. Second, we can move to building deep commitment through agent consensus rather than on bias selling to authority (really a form of upward coercion). And, third, we acknowledge and use emotions rather than submerging them. Events or circumstances generate disappointments, fears, and anger—and these emotions themselves need to become the subject of discussion. If we can make negative experiences and associated emotions discussable, we open tremendous opportunity for all agents to learn, redirect, and release themselves from an often crippling sense of frustration. Finally, even—perhaps especially—things that seem simple and common sense are rich topics for dialogue because they afford an opportunity to work with agents on methods of discovering and carrying out solutions for themselves. Through dialogue, we can help teams to generate comfort with the validity of the information they've generated from their models and metrics and with their ability to act on it.

Over time, it is likely we will be able to replace many of these hierarchical reviews and dialogues with peer reviews, dialogues, and brainstorming. Peers are often privy to the same level of detailed understanding or implications behind our decisions and choices. They are, therefore, the ideal partners to help us ferret out our best course of action. Peer reviews are ideal for agent learning and sharing and should constitute a good portion of our everyday schedule. They're terrific for surfacing change in trends, patterns, and business propositions and enabling people to affirm critical pattern signals for themselves. Peer reviews with a fluid flow of participants contribute substantially to creating a web of more functional patterns.

Even as the designated power hierarchy is removed, there will continue to be enterprise decision makers who earn their positions at all levels, micro to macro. Often, consensus does not emerge fast enough to meet market demands. These leaders will also facilitate the flow of communications about decisions and resources. As the leader role changes and we become practiced in operating within the web structures, we should expect new leader selection techniques to emerge.

Embodying and Communicating Direction

In the late eighteenth century, the United States set up a government-sponsored postal system to promote commercial growth and political and social communication. Despite some of our grumbling today, the Post Office has been inordinately successful. When the Soviet Union set up a postal system in the nineteenth century, it was so that the government could read everyone's mail. They were also successful.

As leaders, we must remember that the purpose behind a structure is as important as the structure itself. What we communicate is a result not only of what we say or write but also—and more important—what objectives we have in mind and what we actually do.

Patterning the Business Web Structure

As leaders test and prove to themselves the generative proposition that business competency is due to interlocking behaviors of many people rather than the expertise of one (or few), we will be better able to help generate weblike organizational structures and patterns. "Simply" by connecting dumb neurons, the human brain becomes smart; and, from the connection of millions of dumb PCs on the Internet, there emerges the amazing power of the World Wide Web. We can make smart humans even smarter through effective connections. Like simple chips imbedded in cars, elevators, and microwaves, by encouraging a few basic memes in all members of our business, we are enabling them to connect in a functional pattern. With use over time, the capabilities of the web improve. Eventually, it becomes impossible for competitors to replicate products and services produced by a business based on a complex web of agents, skills, experience, and relationships.

Words Aren't Enough: A Disguised Vicious Cycle

As Vladimir Ilyich Lenin, who might have been better served by taking his own advice, remarked: "Perhaps the most difficult [thing] is diminishing authority. Authority poisons everybody who takes authority on himself."[2] Some of us will find it very difficult to release control. In the end, if we, as leaders, can't change our personal habits to walk the talk (and not just talk it), we should find a role as an individual contributor.

In this story, Mary Ann talks about the heartbreaking experience of joining a team in which the leader used hypercycle words and concepts but was not, in the end, able to release the command-and-control paradigm. Mary Ann recalls: I joined this team very excited to be working in leading-edge technology and excited about the business unit's desire for the products we were to deliver. Before joining, I spoke with the president of the business and at least 10 people in the field, all of whom expressed an urgent need for the software the team was to deliver. Initial excitement and commitment among team members was very high.

Several months later, however, we were tired and discouraged. Although we participated in dialogue and planning sessions—based on environmental reviews and considering the continuing urgency of development—our plans were severely tightened and rewritten by more senior management—based on desired, not team, capability. "Agreement" to the impossible tighter plans was coerced, and the destructive games began. I'm sorry to report we played chicken; we hoped others would fail; we counted on suppliers to be late; and we started covertly attacking each other. In a context where everything was sold rather than discussed, I began to worry about personal credibility, self-preservation, and my next job. These thoughts warred with my continuing desire to actually produce the product that I still believed in. I worked 14 hours a day. So did most everyone else. When the team was able to meet deadlines, it was mostly through ultimately destructive heroic efforts. Emotions ran high. We were all perpetually exhausted.

The stress affected my marriage (not permanently, I'm happy to say), and friends urged me to get out. Finally, sadly, still mostly committed to the business goal, I left the team. So did others. The project was not completed. It was an enormous waste of terrific ideas, time, talent, funding, emotional energy. Everyone—certainly including the business—lost.

Engaging Agents, Catalysts, and Eco-Technicians

Agents

In a web environment, a key role for leaders is to develop a good team composition—selecting, recruiting, and assembling appropriate diverse players. Some organizations currently testing the applications of complexity science have found agents with generic skills, shared memes, and a positive attitude far more valuable than some of the high-priced specialists they had recruited previously.

Some enterprises, successfully using complexity-based leadership, insist that anyone with time and proper coaching can acclimate to the environment we are espousing. Others report that there are people who find themselves extremely uncomfortable with the transition and new behavior required and who will leave the business (either by personal choice or due to group pressure). These latter companies are developing new screening mechanisms for employment. They rely heavily on personal interviews, as well as temporary consulting assignments, as a form of pilot experience so that both the individual and the organization can assess the fit. When a fit occurs, they sign up to a mutual and deep long-term commitment. The result has been highly successful in both enterprise performance and employee satisfaction.

Often business units have a wealth of talented agents with insufficient focus or motivation to adapt to a new environment. They are already overburdened, asked to produce beyond capability, and to work without any chance to review what they do, develop new approaches, or learn new skills for evolving. In addition, thrashing between competing assignments is a growing problem. Leaders must find a way, with the help of catalysts and eco-technicians, to create a space in which agents can engage the desired changes. A first step in leveraging agent competencies is encouraging teams to measure, understand, document, and inventory their own capabilities and actual performance. Leadership coaching and support for this learning is a critical part of climbing the enterprise fitness peak from level 1 to level 2.

Eventually, if agents are unable to change to the new rules, even with significant help, they must be removed from the team. Many such agents will remove themselves, because they are no longer comfortable in the new environment. And, in some cases, the agent web is so strong that it pushes out peers much as an immune system ejects viral or cancerous "cells." Agents are fully aware when other agents don't share the enterprise memes and are quite capable of forcing them out.

Changes in agent responsibilities often take place not because of agent incompetence, but because the nature of the business or project changes. When an effort or business is closed down, for example, due to changes in market conditions, a careful inventory of webbed skills, experience, and relationships is useful. Astute leaders will assess the opportunity for transplanting linked competencies by feeding a whole unit with new knowledge and perhaps transplanting some complimentary agents to catalyze or nurture the fledgling competence until new roots take hold. Similarly, to make the best use of agents and competency, it is appropriate to review team constituency when an effort moves from initiation or research into pilot, roll-out, or ongoing operation. The composition of the team may need to be adjusted to fit the new tasks.

Finally, leaders need to be clear about the boundaries of autonomy. Being autonomous doesn't necessarily mean do it yourself. As leaders we need to query teams about the various possibilities on the make/buy/borrow/join spectrum. Nor does autonomous mean do it *by* yourself. Projects that are isolated and driven by agents set aside to go it alone often take us into the hidden traps of pet projects, personal agendas, and ultimately invisible risk. At fitness level 3, we need to encourage internal and external scanning and awareness as a critical focus of all agents. This suggests we find ways to reward agents based on their reach and emergent (rather than assigned) influence in the enterprise web.

Selecting Catalysts and Eco-Technicians

Chapter 12 is devoted to the nature of the business catalyst role and Chapter 13 discusses the role of eco-technicians. Because leaders, at least for the time being, are charged with selecting people for these new roles, we have listed the key qualities for each in the roles we envision. Qualities important to organizational catalysts include:

1. Appropriate personal chemistry (for example, temperament and leadership qualities that fit the target unit's organizational paradigm)

2. Some professional knowledge in the target unit's area

3. Breadth of enterprise knowledge

4. Deserving of respect by agents and leaders

5. Ability to coach and act as a mentor for individuals and small groups

6. Presentation and communication skills

7. Ability to listen

8. Some experience with group self-assessment

9. Significant years of professional experience

10. Good at surfacing healthy conflict
11. Nonthreatening style
12. Team player

Qualities important to eco-technicians are (note that the first four qualities are the same):

1. Appropriate personal chemistry (for example, temperament and leadership qualities that fit the target unit's organizational paradigm)
2. Some professional knowledge in the target unit's area
3. Breadth of enterprise knowledge
4. Deserving of respect by agents and leaders
5. Natural grasp of systems approach and theory
6. Investigative skills
7. Problem-solving abilities
8. Training in mathematics and abstract modeling
9. Patience and attention to detail

A Hypercycle Story: Citibank's Corporate Technology Office

In this story, Susanne talks about the powerful and enlightening experience she had participating in a highly effective business unit lead by Colin Crook, then Citibank's senior technology officer (STO). In Susanne's words:

"I joined Citibank's Corporate Technology Office (CTO) in late 1992 to run a program called the *Software Initiative*, which we'll discuss more in Chapters 14 and 15. Briefly, the Citibank Software Initiative was an internal effort to improve the speed, predictability, and effectiveness of internal systems development.

When I joined, I found that the CTO functioned as the most effective hypercycle I'd ever been a part of. As early as my first interview with Colin Crook, there were indications that this experience would be unlike any I had ever had before. In that interview, Colin asked me what percentage of my day I spent 'taking time to think.' I must say I found the question a bit odd. I wondered if he, like me, had ever run a customer service and help desk function for a large data center (which had just taken over the functions of 14 data centers from all over the United States). When did anybody have time to *think*?

The irony of this sticks with me constantly. I wonder how much we are losing in intellectual capital and wasted resources because we don't encourage or even allow time for our people to think! In persistently raising the issue of thinking and thoughtful action, Colin was clear in his message: I knew a major part of my job as a catalyst was to make the time to think and encourage others to do the same.

Colin Crook joined Citibank in 1990 as the STO and head of the CTO with the responsibility of establishing strategic direction for technology throughout the bank. In many areas, however, his position was one of influence rather than control—as all technologists at Citibank reported directly to the businesses they supported with a secondary reporting line to the STO."

Staffing the Corporate Technology Office

The CTO was composed of catalysts and specialists—with each staff member focused on a specific initiative. Leading by example, Colin wanted to propagate the idea of using catalysts throughout the Citibank world. He believed that putting the right catalysts in place was one key way of accelerating corporate change and evolution. And, he considered identifying, activating, and empowering highly effective and independent people one of his most critical responsibilities. By selecting the right people and using the concept of catalysts rather than controllers, Colin was able to staff the technology office of one of the world's largest corporations with fewer than 20 employees.

Those who were already successful in the CTO screened candidates for open positions. In this way, the candidate learned a great deal about the prospective environment from those who knew it best, while the team had the opportunity to assess whether the new player was likely to succeed. I didn't even meet Colin until my potential colleagues had given the OK. In the traditional interview sequence, first the boss selects a candidate, and then prospective colleagues interview the candidate for fit. Reversing the sequence generates true input to the leader, not a rubber stamp from people who know this is the candidate the boss wants to hire.

Though we usually hired well as a team, we didn't fire well: We nearly didn't fire at all. If anything, our Achilles heel in the CTO was our reluctance to remove agents that were ineffective in the hypercycle environment. We didn't have a well-developed immune system among partners, nor was Colin prone to give up on mentoring and coaching even when incurable patterns became evident.

Embodying and Communicating Direction

The Software Initiative was Colin Crook's answer (for Citibank) to a crisis that was raging industrywide. Although widely considered a leader in technology, Citibank's software development process was out of control, chaotic, and a risk to the enterprise.

From the beginning, Colin's behavioral and verbal messages about the Software Initiative were loud, clear, consistent, and unrelenting. He communicated need for evolution and change to a software engineering mentality and more disciplined behavior. He focused on the goal of survival for both the individual agent (to ward off the death knell prophesized in *The Decline and Fall of the American Programmer*[3]) and software development organizations (to compete with outsourcing). In addition to providing information about internal problems, Colin translated, reinforced, and propagated environmental messages providing information about the crisis from the outside. He raised corporate consciousness about the nature and extent of the problem and repositioned Citibank's patterns of memory and history by pointing out old theories and approaches that might have worked once but were no longer effective.

Colin signaled the urgency to technology leaders: We must change or we will be put out of business. As might be expected, Colin set corporate policy and provided catalytic programs in support. But he also set specific goals for continual evolution, which were backed by funding criteria (if your organization has not met a certain level of maturity within three years, your technology budget will not be funded). This generated urgency and put environmental pressure behind the long-term strategic objective of increasing discipline in software engineering—helping it to be equal in priority to short-term project efforts demanded by the business managers.

Developing New Habits

Another early CTO lesson for me had to do with self-discipline and 'fessing-up to a bad habit we leaders tend to exhibit: "Do what I say, not what I do!" At the time, I was still new to the CTO and operating with my old habits in the new context. Having requested a meeting with Colin to provide a project update ("sell" how well I was doing with my initiative), I was proceeding as I had expected until. . . . In the middle of touting the importance of knowing your process and having the self-discipline for habitually making it explicit, then measuring and improving it, Colin stopped me for a question.

"What's *your* process?" he asked in a very quiet, nonthreatening, and matter-of-fact manner.

I was stopped dead in my tracks. Thus prompted on the spot, I discovered I did have a process; I was actually measuring and improving it; *but it wasn't explicit,* so that others could contribute to, join with, or learn from my patterns. We dumped the sales pitch and had a terrific dialogue about my process!

Colin and I found that there were some other old habits and beliefs rattling around driving my process. One that comes to mind was my belief that going to seminars and conferences was a luxury (an expense that did not truly contribute to business success) or a form of recognition for good work. I had not included room for this investment in my process. Colin encouraged contact outside the enterprise for several reasons:

1. To be sure we knew what was going on around us outside the business as well as what longer-term environmental trends were emerging

2. To influence the environmental trends on behalf of the enterprise

3. To build both enterprise and personal credibility, thereby increasing the ability to influence the environment

4. To cycle the external personal reputation internally, enabling more effective personal influence within

Our heads turned by hearsay and reputation, we leaders have a misguided habit of going to external consultants for information about circumstances within our business at times when the people in the actual business circumstances have far more information. With training and encouragement, enterprise agents can have both the skills and credibility to offer deeper insight than visitors. Gaining external ideas, perceptions, models, and an external reputation gives agents more opportunity to provide added value internally. In the Information Age, it is critical for each person to gain knowledge and generate intellectual capital. Powerful agents are a major key to enterprise success.

Reducing the Artificial Power Hierarchy and Engaging Natural Organization

At first my time on the Software Initiative was spent digging into the background of Colin's strategies and speaking to colleagues who had been involved prior to my arrival. We brainstormed about how to integrate my initiative with other CTO efforts so that the synergy of the efforts multiplied the strength we had behind them. I was amazed both at how independently everyone worked while at the same time participating in a web of cooperation, commitment, and information flow. Colin referred to us as his partners, not his staff. It certainly encouraged us to work that way! What a difference this title made. This was a good lesson in ways to reduce the power hierarchy—a lesson later supported by the idea that we humans create and understand our "reality" through our use of language.

Early in my assignment, I'd get a sense of something new that needed to be done, a course of action that needed to be redirected or message that needed to change. I'd put together a plan of action for communication with (mostly selling to) Colin. I expected that we would discuss the proposal, and then he would either approve it or make suggestions. This is what had happened with other managers. In other words, Colin would be the boss and tell me what to do. By doing this, he would share my responsibility.

This was not the case. He asked questions. "Was I comfortable that I had all bases covered?" "Who was my target for X?" "What was my process for interacting with Y?" When we discussed my proposal for selling the Software Initiative to managers based on bottom-line results, he simply asked whether I thought this approach would work with programmer analysts as well, and did it matter whether it did? At the end of the session, he had made no additions, changes, or deletions to my proposal. Instead, he had prompted me with a series of questions that I had the responsibility for considering. This was a very powerful second lesson in removing the power hierarchy. Socratic questioning enables a leader to prompt learning and change, while leaving the responsibility for the project in the hands of the person—the autonomous agent— responsible for it.

As a leader, Colin showed unusual strength in leaving responsibility with his partners. On one occasion, when I was uncomfortable with a decision I had to make, I went to Colin for direction. I presented the options and reviewed the associated advantages and disadvantages.

At the end of my presentation, Colin looked at me and said, "You have all the information well laid out. You know what you want to do. You're closer to the situation than I; therefore, you know far more than I can claim to know. You live with the details every day. Why do you want me to share in accountability for the decision you have to make? What is it you are afraid of? Why do you not feel empowered to make that decision?" A simple but powerful question acknowledging how I felt!

After we discussed my reticence and the fact that there was no further information needed, we were back at the bottom line: I had a decision to make. The third lesson I took away is that full autonomy consists of removing fear but not of letting agents off the hook. Actually, it really feels good to know someone trusts you and then to find out all the things that you're capable of doing on your own.

Autonomy can be very frightening to those that empower as well as to those that are empowered. It is quite reasonable to be concerned when you delegate something critical to someone else, while still feeling you could do it better. It is equally frightening to assume responsibility for a task from someone whom you feel could do it better. Working for someone exceptionally competent can be very motivating or very inhibiting. Because I could share my fears with Colin, his competence challenged me to new heights rather than blocking my way. We humans evolved to and are distinguished by our capability to experience emotions. Acknowledging them can generate additional competence and energy to dramatically influence our actions. We are much more effective when we can leverage emotions through dialogue. The fourth lesson: Empowerment is impossible without a two-way climate of trust and respect, which *enables* us to make use of these critical emotions.

Shaping the Web

Management tracking was a whole new experience for me in the CTO. Although monthly reports were still very much a requirement, short and to the point was the rule. Colin was more interested in the feedback he got on CTO initiatives from people who were affected by them than from the people responsible for propagating them. He walked about close to our customers, scanning his network of technology contacts, listening carefully to everyone from programmer to vice president and integrating their stories.

It was my job to establish and support a web of business agents—other catalysts—to drive the Software Initiative around the globe. I was to provide whatever was needed to help magnify their impact or remove obstacles in their way. Colin scanned his own web of leader agents to gather information about the effectiveness of my catalytic activity. At regular intervals, he gathered observations, interactions, relationships, and probabilities to derive a group picture of reality; he did not rely on self-serving sales presentations from me. I was accountable to those with whom I worked—not just my boss. The fifth lesson in natural organization (based on earned influence and power) was that each autonomous agent is accountable to everyone else in the business—more directly, of course, to those with whom he or she works closely and those for whom he or she creates programs or products.

Stop, Look, and Listen

Particularly when in the role of leader, we must avoid trying to boil the ocean. Many erroneously believe that one can undertake a massive top-down cultural redesign to effect a pervasive change in agent behavior. Even those of us who know better get impatient and think wistfully about magic wands or old-fashioned clubs. We all need to remember that carefully chosen small triggers can result in very large-scale results. Simple incentives and intervention can make a dramatic difference. We must take time to think out our interventions systemically.

"Ready, fire, aim" was a nice fad that effectively moved many enterprises away from analysis paralysis. Now it is time that we encourage people, including ourselves, to "Stop, look, and listen"—to think and to have serious dialogue about possibilities and consequences. Early dialogue surfaces potential misalignment in agent intentions and begins the process of interlocking new behavioral patterns and processes early in the game (before mistakes play out and have to be fixed). Folk wisdom again: An ounce of prevention is worth a pound of cure. We can't be everywhere at once. It is best to help agents develop leading indicators for environmental trends, potential risks, and bottlenecks so that they can scan for and prevent problems themselves. In going with the flow of self-organization, we can put the power of a 4-billion-year, well-tested model to work for us.

Chapter Twelve

Catalysts

Assembling a hypercycle is not a short-term, quick-hit, silver-bullet program. Not for the faint hearted, it is a long and arduous journey. I know: I've been on the road now, literally and figuratively, for five years. The job of a catalyst is demanding; it's exhausting; and at times, it is extremely discouraging and very lonely. But it's also exhilarating and wonderfully rewarding. As a catalyst, I've been called everything from out of my mind to brilliant: a zealot, a fanatic, crazy, a pain in the neck, a pest, a friend, a life saver, and a genius.

—SUSANNE KELLY

Local and Global Catalysts

Genius is one percent inspiration and ninety-nine percent perspiration.

—THOMAS ALVA EDISON[1]

Although we may understand that any process requires energy, if we were to characterize the increased rate of chemical reaction enhanced by a catalyst, we would say that somehow it appears effortless. It just seems to happen. On the business front, effective catalysts sometimes create a similar image. Their years of intense commitment, difficult decisions, and expenditure of personal energy are not obvious to the observer. The real story behind the overnight success of business catalysts is closer to Edison's 99 percent perspiration than it is to the 1 percent inspiration—although that 1 percent is also clearly important in the process.

In this chapter, Susanne tells the story of her five years at Citibank in the role of global catalyst while heading the Software Initiative.

So What's the Job?

My responsibility for the Software Initiative was to help establish ideal conditions for small local changes that would thrive and propagate to produce large global impact. The game plan was to foster an improvement in Citibank's software development efforts in 50 technology units and 5,000 people around the world. We wanted software development to be faster, higher quality, and, most important of all, more predictable.

An exciting thing about being a catalyst is the fact that you never stop learning. Unlike chemical catalysts that generate reactions in the chemicals they touch while themselves remaining unchanged, in my job as corporate catalyst, I've gone through tremendous personal change as well. As a result of all the people I've worked with and our mutual experiences, this project self-organized and emerged as much more than a method for changing software processes.

Although the job title of *catalyst* may be new, the idea is not. We turn again to oral traditions and folk sayings, which are passed from generation to generation because they contain embedded wisdom, with the following:

> Give a man a fish, and he'll eat today.
> Teach him how to fish, and he'll eat tomorrow.

This is exactly the point. The main job of a catalyst is to speed up business evolution by helping autonomous agents to empower, energize, and activate themselves. Among the most difficult aspects is the critical task of removing oneself from each primordial pond and leaving behind an ecology that will sustain itself. Although it may be necessary in the early stages of evolution to assume some authority and to prop up agents and teams that are not ready to stand alone, catalysts know they have been successful when they are no longer needed.

With catalytic opportunities ranging from local to global, catalysts can provide triggering at any of the nested levels within a business organization. A *local* catalyst is only effective in a small unit of autonomous agents, generally ranging from 20 to 40 people. For larger environments, a web of catalysts is required. This web will need its own catalytic energy: a more global catalyst working within nested units, divisions, or businesses.

But What Does a Catalyst Do to Trigger Powerful Changes?

Whether the focus is local or global, the fundamentals are the same. This is a brief overview, which is followed with stories of my experiences in our Citibank global lab.

First, the catalyst develops an awareness of the new sciences and learns not only to apply but also to visibly embody the four simple rules. (I didn't start here, but only wish I had! It would have saved a lot of time and misguided effort.) With ongoing self-assessment and feedback from colleagues, the catalyst embarks on what will become a life-long learning experience.

With a little scientific and self-understanding, the catalyst is ready to stir up a lot of change. Based on the nature of the target pond, catalysts customize appropriate models and tools to be used as a framework for the change process. In the Software Initiative, the Software Engineering Institute's (SEI) Capability Maturity Model (CMM) was readily available.

Conscious catalysts, unlike our chemical counterparts, have the opportunity and responsibility to choose the best primordial pond for jumping into. In the third step, the catalyst selects a target intervention level and unit based on a review of the key ingredients that enable success in group evolution.

When the unit and the catalyst have agreed to proceed, the catalyst begins by providing the group with basic information about the selected framework for change—a professional assessor to assist the group in conducting a self-assessment. Self-assessment is only effective when it is facilitated using an extremely well-defined process.

In the fourth step, the catalyst assists the group in building on the results of the self-assessment. To help everyone co-evolve, the catalyst first helps generate deep commitment to a set of long-term unit goals. Next, visible think-do-check-act scenarios for reaching those goals are put in motion. The catalyst also provides continual training in any models, processes, or tools needed to support change.

Throughout the evolution process, the catalyst ensures that the self-organizing system is fed and reinforced with energy and information: from the unit to the corporation and back to the unit. The catalyst engages in regular dialogue with agents and leaders to revisit and crystallize game plans, maintain the high-level visibility of checkpoints, and encourage the results. Above all else, the catalyst pours in personal, professional, and business energy to maintain the urgency and motivation for getting real things accomplished.

As the unit begins to move from one evolutionary fitness level to another, the catalyst helps to celebrate successes and to connect the unit with other units at similar and, in some cases, more advanced levels. As agents become more autonomous and make the evolutionary model their own, the catalyst turns his or her attention to enabling the agents to become self-sustaining.

Finally, no longer required, the catalyst looks for a new pond in which to start over.

Quicksand and Increasing Returns

Some of the best advice I've ever received was from a friend of mine who was an independent consultant. When she heard that I was embarking on this assignment as an internal management consultant, she said, "Never jump into quicksand. There are such things as bad consulting assignments. Walk away from them. Don't get sucked into problems that people are not willing to work on fixing for themselves."

A catalyst's job is to help people grow and learn to help themselves—not to take on their responsibilities for them. My biggest lesson in making deep commitments was saying no to doing things *for* rather than *with* people. I no longer say yes or even maybe to groups that aren't themselves committed to attacking their own problems. We, as human catalysts, have limited resources (funding, energy, time, and patience) for triggering evolution. We can choose to help people who have the key ingredients in place for success and help make it happen, or take on those who don't and fail with them.

It is rarely a popular decision to walk away from a group, whether or not they think they have problems to fix. I try to tell those groups I walk away from why I am making that decision. Sometimes my honest opinion is enough to get them started on developing their own deep commitment. I'm eager to reverse my opinion and decision to provide support if and when they, themselves, are ready to work as hard as I am.

Catalysts become part of the market selection process, supporting memes that will propagate and flourish or wasting resources on those that will die out. Cost-effective and rapid business change takes place like an epidemic. Those who are most receptive get "infected" first. In turn, those first successfully infected will infect others, who will infect others, and so on. Complexity science labels this the *law of increasing returns.*

Epidemics will spread more rapidly if carriers—such as the infamous Typhoid Mary—either travel or communicate widely across different business areas or geographic sites. Catalysts persist as the business shifts from being primarily command and control to being mostly consciously self-organizing. To outsiders, it may appear to have just happened all of a sudden by itself. It is more accurately described by a concept called the *tipping factor.* When, with help from leaders, catalysts, and eco-technicians, the first unit in a business becomes successful by consciously self-organizing, it can "infect" a second unit. The success of each of these two units then triggers this change in an additional unit and so on. The process may be invisible to anyone other than those directly involved, but the rate of change will be exponential. Eventually, a threshold is reached and the business suddenly *tips* from being primarily command and control to consciously self-organizing.

Five Key Ingredients Enabling Group Evolution

Here are the five ingredients key to reaching the threshold. The odds of success are highest in units that have all five.

The first is *sponsor commitment.* In my view: For the next few years, most catalysts will be working in places driven by a power hierarchy. People look to the "top" for direction. The most critical ingredient, therefore, is a sponsoring senior manager who is deeply committed to the effectiveness of conscious self-organization. Ideally, the CEO is committed to that change, and the whole enterprise environment is targeted for transformation.

In addition to senior support, the catalyst needs commitment from the immediate manager of each target unit. I look for someone who wants to release the power inherent in his or her own organization and understands that single-handed control is not the answer. Immediate managers function as a day-to-day conduit to and buffer for their organization. As a conduit, the manager can provide daily energy behind the four simple rules. At the same time, he or she can buffer the unit from inappropriate pressure in the power hierarchy. Requests such as "just get it done," "tell me what I want to hear," "no need to think, I do the thinking around here," and "we'll be fine as long as you do what I say" are my nightmare examples of power pressures. Local managers committed to change have a beg, borrow, or steal mind-set that supports the process all the way.

Keep a wary eye on the "Ides of March" and the "yes, *but*" mentality. It doesn't much matter whether the local manager is truly committed but in an impossible environment, or shallowly committed and giving lip service. The words "Yes, I'd really like to support this *but . . .* [pick one] I don't have the budget; we're too busy this year; my manager doesn't understand; [or, worse yet] can you quantify the return?" These are all definite danger signs.

Patience goes hand in hand with commitment. Committed managers are *patient* enough to let the unit discover its own problems and appropriate contextual solutions.

The second key ingredient is good *catalysts, themselves.* When working in a large business, if you are to coordinate a web of other catalysts, check them out before jumping in. Often, when a senior-level manager seeks my help, a program of change has already begun; and local catalysts have been assigned.

Some are excellent. Others are really control freaks in disguise. Control freaks want to change their environments single-handedly in *their* way to a paradigm *they've* selected for *their* reality. Usually, they are well-meaning people but nonetheless, they are either misguided or unaware of the nature of self-organization. Appropriate partner catalysts are facilitative, knowledgeable about complexity and evolutionary change, adept at negotiation, and, above all, persistent. You'll recognize them as willing and able partners, removing organizational obstacles that are blocking distributed control, following through on needed agent actions and decisions, and communicating the same informational and motivational messages over and over ad nauseum.

The third key ingredient is a *sense of urgency in the unit.* No one can make people change when they don't want to or feel the need to. When selecting units, it's exciting to find autonomous agents who are frustrated and disillusioned but still seeking a better way and eager to make a difference. Only autonomous agents, who are willing to do so, discover problems at the microlevel and then implement personally owned solutions. Although it isn't necessary that all agents in a unit are open to change, you need a majority of those involved to be committed to the change process. You start with a few on the fringe, bring most of the group on board, and peer pressure will bring in any remaining laggards.

The *environment in which the target unit is nested,* the fourth key ingredient, will make a difference. Just as certain chemical reactions require a specific range of temperature and pressure, units undergoing change require specific environmental support. Unless you are working with an entire business, every organizational unit is nested within a larger corporate entity. If the context is conducive to the change, the change will be easier. If it is hostile, the change at best will be difficult, at worst impossible. Before initiating change in such an environment, it's wise to assess the level and nature of the hostility. Deciding to move forward with change means you and the unit manager will need to partner to shore up the unit boundaries and protect it against the effects of the environment. And this brings us to the fifth and final key ingredient—*boundaries.*

Boundaries are critical to evolution. One of the first things to emerge in the evolution of a cell was the cellular membrane. Specialization in multicellular organisms has been accomplished via the emergence of semipermeable membranes encapsulating the nested system. Acting both as buffers to filter out some types of information and energy or conduits to draw other types in, boundaries are critical.

A natural by-product of our memes, organizational boundaries are formed by patterns of communication and learning behavior. Our boundaries can be supported by or in conflict with structures represented by an organization chart and corporate policies. As individuals or members of groups, we develop our own behavioral boundaries. What we read, whom we talk to, what we listen to, what we focus on, what we learn, what we try, what we avoid, how we spend our time, where we go: These are all the things that limit our focus or help us to expand beyond current horizons.

To shore up the boundaries for a unit, we draw in information that helps expand our horizons in the directions we've chosen for ourselves and repel information that will distract, discourage, or limit and confine us to the status quo. Units can find examples of success in other organizations or focus on change failures and negative messages, using them as reasons not to try as hard.

The Citibank Software Initiative

A Tale of Two Projects

Prior to my joining the Corporate Technology Office in December 1992, a number of pilots had been initiated using the Capability Maturity Model (CMM). In the first quarter of 1993, I conducted a phone survey of the pilot units. After my calls, I visited the two units that seemed to have made the most progress. They were already engaged in change programs and had catalysts in place to help them evolve.

One location had assigned catalyst responsibility to a highly motivated and capable individual who was a self-appointed champion, dedicated to the concepts of organizational evolution. The manager of the unit gave credible lip service to the effort but did not demonstrate strong sponsorship. Within another six months, the champion had folded his tent and left the bank. The project collapsed.

The second unit had also assigned catalytic responsibility to a highly motivated and capable person. In this case, however, the manager was also fully committed to changing the behavior and culture in his organization. And the entire technology unit wanted the change as well. The business unit that they served (were nested in) was active in TQM initiatives, and the business context was conducive to distributed control and agent involvement in change.

In addition, this unit had well-defined boundaries not only based on the strength of their common beliefs but also due to their geographic isolation. Housed in Florida, they were removed from the Citibank corporate concentration in the New York metropolitan area. This means that they were not continually bombarded with a flurry of distractions that could take them off course. I characterized the commitment of this Florida unit as strong.

Their story will help to clarify why they were so well positioned for evolution. During my visit to this unit in January 1993, we discussed what changes they were trying to make in the way they worked together and why they believed those changes were possible. The team members reported that they were evolving because their leader was deeply committed, while the leader said they were evolving because the agents were deeply committed. Everyone agreed it wouldn't be proceeding quite as fast or as well if it weren't for their catalyst, Jennifer Simmons, who kept stirring the pond and getting all the "chemicals" to interact, enabling the emergence of new and changing possibilities. The unit was truly building a self-organizing system, developing a new way of working together.

Jennifer reported that all of the team members were willing to leave their egos on the doorstep when they met. The group was sorting through problems of interaction among themselves and with the people for whom they were creating systems. Jennifer would announce a meeting on a problem topic, and interested parties would join her in getting the issues as well as possible solutions on the table. After the discussion, the person who felt most inclined or in the best position to take a stab at it would walk away with the assignment of drafting a likely solution. They'd reconvene as a group to consider the draft. According to Jennifer, the group could be quite brutal with one another at times. But, before the meetings started, they had acknowledged this might happen and had agreed not to take words uttered in the heat of discussion personally. They had respect for one another and had agreed to mutual coexistence. Agents and leaders alike participated in the meetings as equals; they left rank on the doorstep along with their egos.

Here was a group that was deeply committed enough to engage the evolutionary model in full—with considerable personal energy and effort. I kept asking how all of this came about. We know now that the history of any unit's interactions shape their current structure, memes, and patterns of interaction. Their history, as a unit, made things clear.

About two years previously, the group had been working for a different manager. He made a commitment for them to deliver a rather extensive system in six months, a system the group felt would require more than two years of development. Just two weeks after making that commitment, the manager left the bank to pursue an outside offer. The group was left holding the bag.

When a new manager was hired, he looked at the commitment and realized the discrepancy. He renegotiated as best he could after the fact to deliver about half the system in a year. He had the deep commitment of the group to make good on this promise, and it was a substantial challenge. As they tell the story, they did everything in their power to bring in that system. They worked late nights, weekends, and holidays; family life was sacrificed. Their commitment brought with it stress, serious illness, divorce, and exhaustion. With lots of heroic effort, they rolled out the system in the time to which they had committed. According to them, they were wounded, black-and-blue, and bloody, but proud of this accomplishment.

But, then, in their words: "It was our Vietnam. We came home to no parade. The customer group for the system didn't even say 'thank you.' No one said, 'We appreciate the effort.' All we heard was: 'It took twice as long as it was supposed to and we only got half of what we wanted.' Our group decided then and there that this would never happen again. There simply had to be a better way!"

This unit was able to make difficult change because they were personally committed to improving the quality of their own lives. Many of the units I've worked with since, who have succeeded, have done so because they felt compelled to take responsibility for themselves.

Getting Started on a Broader Basis

With this story in mind, I began looking for other units who were ready to take responsibility for improving their software development environment and their own lives. Although the need was urgent, the response was underwhelming. Because many units were level 1, we required some authority and top management sponsorship to begin.

Colin started the ball rolling by issuing a policy in June 1993 requiring all software development units with a staff of 40 or over to begin an evolutionary program of self-assessment and improvement. In July 1993, I sent a letter to all senior technology managers introducing myself and providing information about the Software Engineering Institute (SEI), including subscription information and details on how to order books and videos about the Capability Maturity Model (CMM). I also requested the name of someone from each organization to act as a catalyst and contact point for the program by the end of the month. I got no responses!

Not to be discouraged, in August I sent a second letter to the senior technology managers thanking all those who responded and asking for a date by which they planned to conduct their self-assessments. Also imbedded in the letter was the fact that the required outside facilitation for each unit self-assessment would run about $28,000 and that I would contribute half of the fee for the first six assessments conducted. (I thought this would capture their attention.) Then the letter went on to provide information about training available at the SEI. Again, I requested a response within a month. And, again, there were no responses by the deadline; but I did receive the first call three days later.

In September, I sent the next letter thanking all those who had responded and reminding those that hadn't that we were still waiting. This time I enclosed a definition of the roles and responsibilities for the catalysts needed to get the program started. Persistence paid off, or maybe people just got back from vacation. At any rate, there was enough interest generated to get started—which means we started conducting self-assessments.

Self-Assessments

From chaos theory, we learned the importance of sensitive dependence on initial conditions and that in living systems the history of the organism cannot be reversed. Each one of us is a biological product of our history, and our current structural coupling determines our ability to interact with our environment. Each environmental interaction changes that coupling. The same is true of groups. So units embarking on conscious change programs need to know exactly where they stand and how they got there. To answer these questions effectively, units need to engage professional (and certified) assessors from outside the group to lead it in a structured process of self-assessment.

The purpose of a unit self-assessment is twofold. First, it is to help agents make visible, have dialogue about, and come to a group understanding of the general starting conditions from which they hope to evolve. Second, the experience of dialogue within the assessment itself begins to change the structural coupling within the group. The open communication, mutual respect, and shared understanding resulting from a well-facilitated self-assessment gives the group a taste of what distributed control and responsibility feel like. If there is a need for change, findings from an assessment will raise the level of urgency as problems are surfaced. Equally as important, it will also identify core competencies to be preserved.

A common understanding of the true nature of the existing business cycle emerges from a good self-assessment. There is no way for people to begin fixing problems if they deny having them. I refer to our model as the five-step program for autonomous agents (AA). Like the other AA (Alcoholics Anonymous), our AA is a self-help program that only works when those who need to change sign themselves in. They do so by committing to a formal self-assessment.

Triggering Not Doing

Some new catalysts take to the role like ducks to water. For others, getting started is quite a challenge. Many assigned a catalyst role fall into the trap of personally writing new procedures for the unit—as opposed to assisting the team in making current behaviors visible and helping them engage in the four simple rules. It is easy to measure physical results in pounds of paper documenting new procedures. Unenlightened managers and catalysts look for results in the wrong media. We don't want changes to paper; we want evolution in behavior. Some may find the blanket of paper comforting and reassuring. I see it as just a place to hide. As catalysts, we must work with eco-technicians to find or develop useful models, measures, and indicators of behavior change so we can monitor our own catalytic effectiveness in helping the unit to evolve.

Part of my corporate catalyst job was to energize or help additional catalysts to evolve. When working with new units, I'd always suggest that they assign someone in their own shop to keep their initiative charged with energy. Supporting *without doing* for others, including other catalysts, is like walking a tightrope. This story provides an example of enabling instead of inadvertently propagating bureaucracy.

A catalyst I was supporting—let's name him Joe—called one day and asked: "Susanne, could you send me a copy of another group's plan for their initiative?"

"What is it you're looking for?" I asked.

"I want to know what you consider an acceptable plan," Joe replied.

"I consider a plan acceptable if it reflects the actions and interactions your unit is going to undertake to accomplish what you need to accomplish," I responded.

"Yeah, but I don't know how much detail you want," he replied.

"It's not about me wanting detail," I protested. "It's about how much detail you folks need to understand among yourselves whatever it is you need to do."

"Well, anyway," he persisted, "will you just send me a plan?"

"No." I responded, as pleasantly as I could.

"Why not?" By then, he'd really gotten annoyed.

"Because this isn't about copying a piece of paper so you can say you have a plan." I was losing it as well. I got a firm grip on myself and tried again: "Here's what I'll do. I'll give you the names of five other people who have created plans. I suggest that you call them and talk to them about their experience in creating those plans. Ask them: 'How did they do it?' 'What problems did they have?' 'What would they do now if they could do it over?' 'What parts of their plans aren't working?' Etcetera, etcetera."

"Why don't you just send me the five plans?" he asked.

He just didn't get it. The experience of working together, not the piece of paper, was the target. In addition, I wanted him to link what his unit was doing with what others were doing. I wanted him to help his unit create a useful map for *themselves,* not something they thought would please the corporate office. I wanted them to think about what they really needed.

An hour later, Joe's boss called me to say, "Why won't you give Joe any help on our plans?" I knew we had a long road ahead. It was over a year before Joe cornered me at a meeting we were both attending.

"I finally figured out what you've been doing," he said a bit sheepishly. "Boy, am I dense! I've learned so much—and all along I've been cursing you for not being helpful."

Allocating Catalytic Time and Resources: An Example at the Corporate Level

As shown in the biosphere experiments, the ecological balance of ingredients has to be right for any system to become self-perpetuating. Catalysts can measure the five key ingredients enabling group evolution—leaders, agents, catalysts, environmental context, and boundaries—to determine where their attention will be most useful. For catalysts whose time and attention are centered on a single group, fitness and progress measures of each ingredient will enable you to focus on and celebrate wins, as well as put more attention on areas that are lagging behind. Catalysts functioning at an overarching nested level, responsible for triggering actions in other catalysts and many units, can use a combined score to decide which of the many catalysts and units will receive needed attention. Susanne describes her experience in this area.

During the Software Initiative, I used a simple grading scale, A to E, to allocate my time and resources. A's got the most attention, E's the least. The goal of a catalyst is to infect the organization with an epidemic of positive change. Just as a virus takes off in a ready host, we must look for the same opportunity in the units we support.

I gave an A rating to any unit that had already made one step up the fitness landscape. This meant all key ingredients were in place and evolution had begun. These units had the most chance of reaching the next peak in the landscape or even leaping to a new landscape. My focus for A's was to assist in their celebrations and then to publicize and build on their success. It is important to invest in these units to help develop a new breed ahead of the pack. Their success helps others to persist when the going is really tough. I recognized their expertise, invited unit representatives to special meetings to emphasize the importance of what they'd done, suggested their names as speakers to address other units, and singled out the leaders for recognition in public forums.

I labeled those units that I believed would become the mainstay of the organization with a B. They had all critical success factors in place and were positioned to progress up the fitness landscape. All they needed was a little time. Actions that I took with B's included providing consulting support to and training opportunities for agents, giving "ata-boys" or "ata-girls" to leaders, listening to catalysts and leaders vent, and setting up contacts with other catalysts and leaders who had solved or were solving the same issues. Most of my time and money went to these units and their catalysts. A significant number of trained catalysts with assessor credentials were—and are—needed to tip a company as large as Citibank. I provided catalysts with opportunities to discover new ideas and workable approaches through visits to other units as instructors and assessors.

Because they were missing one of the critical success factors, units with a fatal flaw received a C rating. These were internal species that, although struggling to evolve, were still stuck in the status quo. The focus of my activity for C's is obvious: I helped them to remove their fatal flaws. For example, in one unit I helped the leader to let go; in another, I coached a catalyst on supporting rather than doing; and in a third, I helped agents to develop a sense of urgency. I used education, coaching, and reading materials. Investment happened in this category as time and money allowed. When the intervention worked and the unit made progress on its own, then I provided additional support.

A grade of D went to units that paid lip service to evolution. These were Citibank's endangered species, characterized by a lot of "yes-buts." The best use of my energy was to take no action with D's. It may seem harsh, but I learned not to waste a minute of time. These units got serious when they thought it was politically correct or when the other groups were progressing and they began to realize that they were endangered. In some cases it was too late, but I couldn't help them change until they were ready.

E-level groups didn't even pay lip service to evolution. Whether they saw it or not, they were inching toward extinction. Blatantly antagonistic and publicly vocal as to what a waste of time any continual change program was, they looked for quick answers to problem symptoms without the underlying discipline, urgency, and agent accountability to pull off any leap to a new peak. What was my action for E's? I suggested that our audit group check them out. If the unit was that opposed to change, chances were that their procedures hadn't been altered in years, that everyone was improvising, and that their shop was out of control. I let Audit provide them with the impetus to change or self-destruct.

The Self-Sustaining Software Initiative

I'd been working on the Software Initiative for a while when Kim Fix, a catalyst working in the Global Relationship Bank, called and said: "Susanne, why don't you get together a forum from around the bank of all the people working this initiative?"

Until this time, I had been getting catalysts started in their respective units and felt they first needed to discover enough about their own environmental issues before being ready for meaningful dialogue with others. I'd put different people in contact with one another as the right opportunities presented themselves but hadn't assembled the group as a whole.

"That's a great idea," I replied. "Why don't you do it? I'll help. You know better than I do what you would like to talk about and accomplish."

Kim's been doing it ever since. It was her idea and her creation; she holds herself accountable. Others love the forum. Kim feels the pride in her accomplishment *and* has the benefit of its work. Bob started a shared database for lessons learned, and Bruce mails out relevant articles. Each time, my only contribution has been, "That's a great idea. Why don't you do it?"

By the end of 1997, my part in the Software Initiative had pretty much wound down to nothing. Catalysts throughout Citibank working on the CMM model have formed their own autocatalytic loops and are keeping the initiative alive without me. Meeting one of the goals of any catalyst, I had worked my way out of a job. I'm not—and shouldn't be— needed. Time for a new position. And here I am, trying to bring to life the complexity-based system of organizational leadership, doing concrete business research, coauthoring this book, and networking with outside complexity catalysts who may have additional ideas to offer us here at Citibank.

And What Would I Do Differently?

I am often asked what I would do differently with the Software Initiative if I could do it over again. The answer is easy: I'd get more grounding in complexity, self-organizing systems, and basic concepts in biological evolution before trying to help groups of people evolve.

Even though the Capability Maturity Model (CMM) is described as an evolutionary model, I missed the point for over a year. I attempted to use old techniques in a job that needed new thinking. I read the model, thought it was a checklist for software technicians, and totally missed the many behavioral lessons inherent in this extremely robust framework. Finally, in the second quarter of 1994, I went to a CMM class at the Software Engineering Institute (SEI). Only then did I realize—so I thought at the time—how much I had missed in the model. I learned that its clarity hid remarkable richness.

Then, in June 1994, I worked with Donna Dunaway and Will Hayes of the SEI to pilot a new self-assessment method called the CBA IPI (*CMM-based appraisal for internal process improvement*). That's when I got another inkling of how much I still had to learn about the model. After becoming certified as a lead assessor, I thought just maybe I had this model under my belt (not so). In the third quarter of 1994, I was invited to work with Mark Paulk and Mary Beth Chrisis of the SEI, along with some others from Motorola, to develop CMM course licensing material for outside of the SEI. Now I was sure I had developed a reasonable comprehension of the CMM. Wrong again. I became a licensed instructor for the CMM material and piloted the class at Citibank. One class was all it took for me to realize how green I still was. About 30 classes later, with significant grounding in complexity thinking, I think I have the basics needed to become a decent catalyst. There's still so much to learn!

Testing Change Models Against the New Sciences

We catalysts (and others) need to be wary of the newest fad literature and models designed for change agents. Before using models that are reputed to work, worked for others, or have great advertising, examine them in light of the concepts from new sciences. Some will work as is, some will need to be tweaked, and some will need to be discarded.

A number of "maturity models" are now being offered by the SEI and other consulting organizations. Before adopting or adapting any of them, evaluate each carefully. Some may not adhere to the evolutionary framework of the software CMM, may not be produced through industry history and professional consensus, or may not advocate an agent self-discovery implementation. Even more disturbing, some newer "over-arching" integrated maturity models are being advocated and developed top-down, macro to micro. These are in direct conflict with concepts of complexity science and the methods we are advocating in this book.

An unfounded assumption, central to many change models, is that most people dislike change and naturally resist it. Yet, we change with every interaction. If we stop changing at a cellular level, we die. In a fractal universe where patterns are repeated at many levels, it doesn't seem logical that we humans would consciously resist and reject change. The concept of bounded instability suggests that a tension between chaos and stability is natural.

We humans may like some changes and dislike others—but any major change is likely to trigger a multistep process that requires time for an interchange of energy and information to adjust our system to its new context. We gather information about it, think about it, put it in a personal context, define our feelings about it and, in doing so, adjust our structures, behaviors, and patterns. Just ask anyone who is newly married.

Many of the models we have examined for our work and consulting do not stand up as well as others. Here's an example.

Changes in Business Situations

A frequently used change model or metaphor looks like Figure 12.1. Contrast this with complexity-based metaphors of bounded instabilities and fitness landscapes. There's a significant difference between a "frozen" business approach and a more fluid position on fitness landscapes. If we don't think in terms of being frozen, we will be less rigid and begin to expect continual change as a part of our environment. There is no freezing and unfreezing involved.

While applying the complexity concepts to models, we must also remember that each situation is unique. Local, practical experience and common sense not only count, they're 99 percent of the game.

The Tricks of the Trade

We assembled these tricks of the trade from the skinned knees of many catalysts.

UNFREEZE   **CHANGE**   **REFREEZE**

FIGURE 12.1
Old Change Model.

1. Begin by providing information, methods of communication, motivation, education, and opportunities for self-discovery, while reinforcing the themes of discipline, integrity, deep commitment, mutual respect, and trust.

2. Use leader authority to initiate evolution in organizations that are not yet high enough up on the fitness landscape to start their own journey. But be careful not to resort to control, edicts, or long-term compliance mechanisms that remove responsibility from where it belongs. Consider any authority you've been given as borrowed and have both personal and professional plans for returning agent responsibility and accountability to its rightful owner.

3. Hold as many classes as you can. In addition to an opportunity for catalyst teaching and the spreading of memes, the classroom is a wonderful place for catalyst learning. We can never hear too much about local reality or gather too much information about how to make our programs more effective: What are people's concerns? What issues do they face every day? Where are they seeking help? What are the key memes already in place? What does the history of each unit bring to the table?

4. Increase the number of catalysts in your business at every opportunity. Share everything you know and work to put yourself out of a job rather than worrying about self-protection and job security. Learn from every catalyst you meet. In a rapidly changing environment, good catalysts are needed everywhere.

5. Establish critical information and feedback loops with other catalysts. Businesswide evolution is spurred on by an active network of cooperative yet competitive catalysts. Catalysts need colleagues with whom they can blow off steam and from whom they can get help. Remembering that emotion is a critical catalytic force, catalysts should make opportunities to celebrate and commiserate with one another. Even a little bit of one-upmanship doesn't hurt ("I'll bet you haven't had this happen. . . ." "Yes, but can you believe . . . ?" "My job's the hardest; I have to deal with. . . .").

6. Many catalysts find a tit-for-tat model of cooperation is effective with the unit(s) they are helping to evolve. They help themselves; you help them. They stop helping themselves; you do the same. The pattern soon becomes clear—especially when you tell them this is exactly what you're doing—and puts the responsibility where it belongs.

7. Test and apply methods to conserve your own scarce resources—especially your energy. The tit-for-tat strategy is one way. Another, especially if you are working at the corporate level, is to actually charge units for your help. Absurd or not, human beings frequently take the things that they pay for more seriously than those that they don't. By charging for the Software Initiative, Susanne's effort became self-funding, something unheard of for corporate staff. When there was more demand than capacity available, it was easy to make the case for acquiring more catalytic resources.

8. Be single-minded about agent *self*-regulation through distribution of responsibility and local decision making. This is a hard one. Because we have lived so long with a Newtonian paradigm, even those of us who try to work in a context of self-organization regress without thinking. Watch out for global "how to" rules, mandatory acceptance of best practices, and forced procedural consistency. Advocate a little messiness and local variation for resilience, flexibility, and ability to co-evolve within context.

9. Expand your perspective by maintaining an active professional life outside the business in which you are employed. There are a lot of opportunities, such as professional organizations, conferences and training programs, speaking engagements, writing, and graduate school. There are a number of good reasons for expanding your professional life in these ways. First, working outside enriches the knowledge, experiences, and tools you apply internally. Second, outside recognition works a special magic in getting insiders to accept more of your help. In addition, working outside is often fun and refreshing, which results

in renewed energy for the tasks at hand. And, finally, because most of us will not work at only one place during our lives, a network of outside contacts provides a realistic view of our options.

Susanne reports that she learned to use this technique effectively. "As I used the Software Engineering Institute's Capability Maturity Model (CMM) as the fundamental model for the Software Initiative, in addition to working closely with the staff at Carnegie Mellon, I linked up with others using the model and accepted speaking engagements to share our experience at Citibank. In time, I was elected to the CMM Advisory Board at the Software Engineering Institute; and, finally, I was encouraged to write this book. In each case, I've learned a lot; I always return to my project richer in catalytic material than when I left."

Chapter Thirteen

Eco-Technicians

It is perhaps not an overstatement to say that sustainable human development is unrealistic without major reliance on information technology.
—ANDREW SAGE, "TOWARD SYSTEMS ECOLOGY"[1]

E co-technicians use the power of technology and complexity-based mathematical modeling and simulation to provide us with a "quantitative mirror" through which we can see ourselves as clearly as possible. With the exception of a few consulting firms in this area, the eco-technician function is nonexistent in most businesses. For businesses that want to fully engage the complexity advantage, this position is as essential to success as the positions of leader and catalyst and not to be confused with our ever-present financial accountants. The eco-technician combines the full strength of scientific theory, mathematics, computing power, and visualization techniques to show the dynamic structure and patterns of the organization as it co-evolves with changing fitness landscapes. At every scale—from the conscious individual nested in a team within a unit within an organization to the business market and global economy—eco-technicians track and promote evolutionary fitness using new tools that take complexity theories into account.

Ecologists and Technicians . . . and Artists

Eco-technicians—eco-techs for short—help us to better see and understand ourselves and our environment. They show us:

- *Our boundaries*

- *The flows of energy, information, and material that cross these boundaries*

- *Our internal and external structural coupling (interlocking patterns of behavior and processes)*

- *The changing fitness landscapes—the ecologies—in which we function*

This is only the beginning.

With useful models in hand, leaders and agents then request parameter changes to run various simulations or scenarios against a variety of fitness landscapes. The "answers" provided by these tools will, of course, prompt new questions. We need not only technicians who understand the science and math but also business ecologists who understand complex business patterns. We need creative thinkers and problem solvers who can use both mathematics and intuition to describe, predict, and influence the key variables in emergent business dynamics.

Any eco-tech who has created an effective business model or simulated scenario faces the challenge of presenting the resulting information clearly. An effective eco-tech will generate a systems-based information ecology that mirrors the business ecology he or she serves. Professor Tom Davenport at the University of Texas in Austin[2] suggests that an effective information ecology:

- *Integrates diverse types of information*

- *Recognizes evolutionary change*

- *Emphasizes observation and description*
- *Focuses on people and their information behavior*

All This and Artists, Too?

With overwhelming volumes of information already coming our way, the need becomes clear for eco-technicians who are also artists. As Marshall McLuhan[3] wrote:

> The power of the arts to anticipate future social and technological developments, by a generation and more, has long been recognized. In this century, Ezra Pound called the artist "the antennae of the race. . . ."

Businesses need eco-techs who can create *elegant and simple models* predicting those patterns most essential to our success and clearly indicating points of opportunity or threat. It is no longer sufficient for mathematicians to track what has happened. We need artists who give us some insight into the future.

Examples of Some of the Tools Eco-Techs Use

Here are just three examples of the many tools that eco-techs use. Notice that they are all methods of making patterns and patterns of interaction visible. Fitness landscapes and spaces of possibilities, which we discussed in Chapter 3, provide a background for almost all eco-tech work.

Power Laws

Power laws describe a circumstance when one quantity can be expressed as a power of another quantity. Power law relationships occur frequently in both nature and business settings (for example, in the motion of the planets around the sun, and in the behavior of consumers with respect to income, consumption, and wealth). Power law capabilities are readily available in industry and appear as a straight line on a double logarithmic plot, *making the pattern very evident*—a key accomplishment for eco-techs. Readers will probably not be surprised to learn that fractals are an expression of power laws.

Patches

A combination problem is one in which there are conflicting constraints in the microsystems of a macrosystem for which a mathematician is trying to find the optimal solution. In a very simple example, the cargo bay of an airplane may need to be very strong to carry highly profitable heavy cargo. This constraint may be in conflict with an overall constraint, however, that calls for the frame of the plane to be as light as possible.

Although patching may not yield the optimal solution to a problem (frequently that takes too long and costs too much), breaking the problem into medium-sized nonoverlapping patches with no individual conflicting constraints enables the solutions in each patch to be optimized. By joining solutions in neighboring patches, these patches will act like co-evolving ecosystems. Excellent, if not optimal, solutions for the entire problem arise in a reasonable time.

Cellular Automata

This tool is exactly what it sounds like: a program that simulates the behavior of cells over time. Automated biological cell models (computer simulations) enable biologists to create simulations designed to examine the evolutionary changes that might take place in various chemical structures, processes, and transformations.

Applying these techniques to business communities, eco-techs can make use of special computer-graphics programs to display three-dimensional images of participants and relationships, showing changes that result when new products or players are introduced.

So If I Want to Be—or to Hire—an Eco-Tech, What Do I Look For?

There is no single template to follow in developing or identifying good eco-technicians. Effective eco-techs can come from a wide variety of backgrounds, with formal education ranging from physics to psychology or even the arts. In most cases, however, both education and experience will be multidisciplinary. We can also look for five key skills that eco-techs need to generate an effective and evolving information ecology. Eco-techs are good at:

1. Identifying patterns and constructing models and scenarios
2. Surfacing emergent networks, connections, and ecologies
3. Recognizing boundaries, inflows and outflows, and feedback systems
4. Determining factors, parameters, leverage points for maintaining bounded instability
5. Providing quantitative training, tools, and coaching to leaders and catalysts

Identifying Patterns and Constructing Models and Scenarios

Eco-techs make full use of mathematical and computer-based graphics to provide visible representations of complex situations.

Eco-tech tools should form an integrated ecology in themselves. As Professor Sage puts it, ". . . without a cohesive systems ecology to guide the use of information, how can we expect to manage today's complex systems?"[4] Sage suggests that a systems ecology comprises:

- *Information technology and information ecology*
- *Industrial ecology and systems engineering*
- *The new and evolving science of complexity*

"Such a systems ecology would enable the modeling, simulation, and management of truly large systems and knowledge, technology, humans, organizations, and the environment that surrounds them."[5]

Providing an Infrastructure for Emergent Networks and Ecologies

An effective eco-tech not only provides models but also assists leaders and teams in engaging the four simple rules by developing effective methods of organizational interaction. Enabling easy and effective communication and connection is a primary eco-tech responsibility. This includes insuring both compatible and easy-to-use communications tools (phones, videoconferences, fax, e-mail, face-to-face meetings housed in places that promote collaboration) and visibly leading the way in building resource networks.

Ecologies—especially those populated with autonomous agents—can be polluted or depleted of resources, leading to stagnation for all who inhabit them. Eco-techs have the responsibility of helping us to replenish our resources so that we can sustain ourselves and those who follow. Ideas from ecology—sustainability, diversity, networks, recycling (of teams, people, memes, equipment), balance, and flexibility—provide a starting checklist of focus areas for the eco-tech.

Maintaining Boundaries, Inflows and Outflows, and Feedback Systems

As businesses restructure, we imply new boundaries and connections for each person and team. Traditional organizational documentation, however, rarely shows flows of energy and resources or emergent structural couplings. Eco-technicians identify and monitor changing nested and intersecting system boundaries as well as the connections across boundaries. They model the energy (business funding and cooperative or competitive effort) and information entering and leaving each system. Too little information handicaps the system; too much overloads it and can be both wasteful and harmful. Making inflows and outflows visible is useful in developing connections and reducing overlap in an evolving structure.

To evolve our fitness we need feedback on our actions. Eco-techs must provide an effective conduit for this feedback. The better and faster we understand both internal and external feedback, the more likely we are to move higher on our fitness peaks or to determine that new peaks are emerging.

Facilitating Bounded Instability

Bounded instability is key to emergent self-organization. Part of the eco-tech's job is assisting in organizational tracking along a series of continua—neither completely fixed and stable nor completely chaotic. If things appear to be too fixed, an eco-tech seeks data that might indicate useful variability. If they are too chaotic or diverse, the eco-tech makes visible potential coupling for increasing order and stability.

As fitness landscapes evolve, new amplifying and balancing feedback loops may be applicable. During product development, for example, shared learning may be the priority. However, during production, that priority may shift to visible execution. Using the four simple rules, an eco-tech helps the team to fuel the appropriate mix of feedback loops.

Teaching, Tools, and Coaching

Finally, eco-techs must have a broad understanding of interactions and interrelations between humans and technology. It is not sufficient for an eco-tech to perform "magic" in a closet, presenting "answers" and "solutions" drawn out of a hat. He or she must be able to bring others along in the process, enabling them to challenge, add to, and modify emerging solutions—making them the team's approach and *not the eco-tech's "answer"* served on a plate and pasted on.

It is not just a matter of making the data available; eco-techs must facilitate understanding and use of the models and scenarios and group decision-making surrounding their use. This demands critical attention to the information needs of humans in problem-solving tasks and the ways in which humans use technology to facilitate their processes. It means sharing tools, arranging for training, and then coaching on the job . . . in effect, helping all of us to become intelligent users of eco-technology.

Evaluating Eco-Technician Effectiveness

The most effective eco-techs will make both direct (linear) and indirect (nonlinear) contributions to the enterprise. The nonlinear effects are likely to be more powerful but harder to measure in traditional ways. One clear point of eco-tech assessment is their support of the business or team as it moves up the evolutionary fitness model. Another is the value or contribution of their "out-of-the box" solutions. A third is the assessment of the eco-tech's personal effectiveness as determined by the business or team he or she supports.

An Interview with a Rare Species: Real Live Eco-Technicians

Originally founded in June 1995, CASA (Center for Adaptive Systems Applications)[6] is a for-profit, privately owned firm of eco-technicians located in Los Alamos, New Mexico. CASA's initial major relationship with Citibank started in July 1995. CASA now provides services not only to Citibank, but also to a variety of other businesses. When we introduced the job title, *eco-technician,* they said: "That's us; that's exactly what we do." We spoke with:

- *Steve Coggeshall, a CASA eco-tech who develops models of human behavior usually, but not always, as consumers. A physicist and a practicing orchestra conductor, Steve, who is tall with a medium build and a bright personality, engages clients in innovative solutions.*

208

- *John Davies, a director at CASA, describes himself as a catalyst and leader in connecting scientists and businesspeople. John is short, almost bald, energetic, and gregarious; his colleagues describe him as Puckish in the positive sense.*

- *Camilo Gomez, a CASA eco-tech, develops models of investments and balance sheets as well as overall corporate behavior. Camilo is of medium height with dark hair. Although the youngest of the three, he has been a Wall Street trader as well as a practical physicist.*

What Do You—As Some of the World's First Eco-Techs—Actually Do?

Steve led off by saying: "We find new ways of looking at things."

Camilo added, "We combine ecology and technology for businesses. The underlying fabric of any business must be addressed in order for that business to function effectively. By weaving technology into the memes that already exist in a business, we improve the fabric. We investigate and model the ecology of the business."

John emphasized this idea: "I think of CASA as joining the business—forming an ecology with our client businesses." He went on, "We start by looking at any problem by running several scenarios. We inject new ways of thinking and new processes into an organization. We're not eco-techs when we apply preset solutions, even if they are effective."

Camilo: "We help with managing under uncertainty. CASA runs both simulations (showing potential results of rule-driven processes) and modeling (hypothetical results based on data and statistics). If there's not enough information to create a model which enables projections, there are tools which can help anyway: tools which help leaders to reduce uncertainty and select the most robust options among a series of possible actions."

Experiences with Businesses So Far

John: "Frequently when we come into a new organization, there's an antibody reaction—the system just works naturally to push us out because we are different."

Steve: "Many business ecologies are self-limiting. You must be able to take risks in order to change."

John: "Eco-techs face the paradox of needing to be integrated tightly in the organization while at the same time remaining able to stand back and to disengage in order to see the macrolevel."

Steve: "If we're not well connected enough, we'll invent visions that are not practical. It is very important to engage at both senior management and day-to-day business levels in order to create innovative tools that work."

Camilo: "Sometimes when we start working with a business, people just seem to get it; other times they don't get it at all. Those more senior in the organization tend to have more of a complexity perspective and to think more broadly, this is less so of managers in an individual business silo."

John: "We have to live together for a while in a client domain. When it really works right, we form an ecology with that client."

Camilo added: "Internal corporate turnover is a problem for us. When we lose someone who really understands, we have to start over again."

Where Should Eco-Techs Focus?

Camilo: "In order to be effective, eco-techs should be placed at the highest levels of the organization. This is the place where real structural and out-of-the box changes can take place. If we start lower in the organization, it often reduces our effectiveness."

John: "We're most effective at modeling macroprocesses and patterns. We must be able to stand back and look at the whole organization."

Steve: "The complexity concepts come from the top . . . but we *must* be able to work with people on the front lines; they know the detailed reality. And many detailed people have excellent vision."

Camilo: "In order to be effective at any level, we *must have* buy-in from the lower levels. We need the information and expert knowledge only they can give us."

Steve: "Eco-techs must operate in both realms. It's our role to help bring alignment between the micro and the macro. This provides the opening for us to locate those cross-business opportunities that are hard to find when your task is to manage one area and focus only one to two quarters out."

Eco-Tech Contributions

John: "Our contributions are hard to evaluate. They often include making judgments about long-term direction. They are imbedded in the patterns of the organization. We frequently solve problems and identify opportunities beyond the scope of those we're brought in to address. Not doing what we set out to do might be considered a failure in the traditional sense, although we're still adding value."

Camilo: "We often enable the implementation of simple non-complex techniques to handle problem situations. However, finding that simple solution required us to use highly complex techniques, often modeled in many dimensions."

Steve: "Another problem is that frequently, when we find a simple solution, it looks obvious and people tend to downplay the effort it took to reach it. Think of one of John Cage's musical compositions which features "silence." Reproducing this composition is very easy. Thinking of it took a very different mind-set."

John: "This is a new way to think."

Placing a Value on Eco-Tech Contributions

Camilo: "Because we live in an environment with such a high premium on shareholder value, it is hard for CEOs and companies to take long-term risks. The business world's quarter-to-quarter performance makes pursuing longer-term trends more difficult."

John: "We do have some strategy-oriented models—one in particular—that helps management show the benefits of a more self-sustaining approach. We are working to validate them."

Steve: "We frequently solve something other than the original problem. People aren't used to paying for something other than what they asked for!"

John: "If we have to think against a specific problem, in a business silo, not in strategies, we could miss the whole thing. We might solve that problem and save 50,000 dollars," again a pause to emphasize the consequences, "but miss a related opportunity to create a new product line that makes a billion."

Steve: "Sometimes we're almost too successful. People are so busy using the initial solution that they don't want to hear about changes and continuing evolution."

Camilo: "We also have to be willing to admit that the area in question doesn't require a complexity-based solution. This one is really important."

Tell Us About Other Eco-Techs

There was a long pause, then John said: "We know of several other consulting companies that are starting to do eco-tech work."

Steve: "Because their boundaries are so strong and their thinking is so bureaucratic, governments are the furthest from having and using eco-techs."

Steve: "Although some academics understand the theories, many don't turn this understanding inward to their own organizations. There are academics, including some at MIT, Michigan, Northwestern, and Stanford, who consult with business and are deeply grounded in reality; they have to be."

Characteristics of Good Eco-Techs

Based on their experience, we asked Steve, John, and Camilo to tell us what characteristics helped some to be a successful eco-technician. Here's a summary of what they said. An eco-tech must be:

- *Very curious and able to soak up details like a sponge*
- *Fluid and able to think easily in a nonlinear way*
- *Able to think in more than one dimension—preferably in three or more dimensions*
- *A risk taker who is highly intuitive and not afraid to think in new ways*

- *A multidisciplinary thinker with a multicultural perspective*

- *Educated in both a technical area (usually physics) and some form of psychology*

- *Able to move from business to business easily and to uncover structural coupling in any type of organization*

- *Able to model human behavior and real "messy" interactive processes (not just tidy abstractions and sequential step processes)*

- *Always trying to find global rules*

- *Able to deal with people effectively*

- *Interested in and capable of producing hard results—very practical*

Save Your Money: Be Sure You've Attained Fitness Level 3 Before Focusing on Level 4

Before we, as leaders, rush out to position eco-techs throughout our businesses, we need to reflect carefully on where we (our units) are against the complexity advantage evolutionary fitness model. If we are still at levels 1 or 2, we will probably waste time and money investing extensively in eco-techs. Only when we are solidly at level 3 are teams able to understand clearly what they do and, therefore, *to make use of models and scenarios to adapt their patterns of interaction.*

During the CASA interview, John Davies commented: "There's some question, still, I think, about whether eco-techs are even effective *inside* a corporation. There's a tendency to *un*eco-tech them . . . to put them in a box . . ." he paused for emphasis, "which makes them less effective. When eco-techs are normalized, when they are forced to solve an isolated specific problem—and only that problem (not problems in the related context)—they lose their true effectiveness."

We don't think there is any question about whether eco-technicians can and should play major roles in businesses. We do think there is a point of readiness, which is during the move from level 3 to level 4. We use complexity advantage step 11—adopt statistical thinking, nonlinear mathematics, and complexity models for insight—to move to level 4. Level 4 is the first time we have the ability to focus effectively at both the micro- and macrolevels simultaneously and, thereby, to engage the full capacity of effective eco-technicians.

As John said, "This [eco-tech] is a new way to think. And, at the right level of fitness, eco-techs are vital to a business's ability to compete effectively."

•

The New Breed of Business

Chapter Fourteen

Experiencing the Advantage

*I couldn't go back now to a Level One
organization again. I couldn't survive. You get
used to the order, Level One is too chaotic
and hard to live with.*
—PAUL DOELGER, CORPORATE FINANCIAL
SYSTEMS SOFTWARE QUALITY ASSURANCE

*Here you're able to do what's right for
yourself and for your organization. I've been
shocked at just how good it feels to have this
autonomy, ability, and . . . power!*
—SILVANA LIPOVAC, SOFTWARE ENGINEERING
PROCESS IMPROVEMENT CATALYST

What does the process of developing constructive co-evolutionary fitness sound like in real life? In this chapter we hear from two software teams who work at Citibank about their experiences in the early stages of an evolutionary fitness model.

This chapter originally had long introductions with lots of statistics and history and was, to take liberties in a quotation from William Shakespeare, "full of sound and fury, and signified—well maybe not—nothing"[1] but was not as important as we might have thought. After we had finished interviewing these teams, we decided these remarks should come straight from the horse's mouth. The only changes we made were to take out the "um's" we all have in our actual day-to-day speech, to insert some definitions when we thought the local language—Citispeak—might be unintelligible to anyone other than Citibankers, and to organize the observations according to the complexity advantage four simple rules.

We want to thank these Citibankers for making the time to share their experiences and agreeing to let them be published, and we want our readers to know that those quoted have had the opportunity to read what we wrote and make corrections. So, this is the straight story.

Simple Rule 1: Trust

We made our people a promise. . . . It put people in a position of power.
—SIDNEY GOTTESMAN, LEAD DIRECTOR
OF FINANCIAL POSTING SYSTEMS

"To me, the most important hurdle is the rejection of being a victim. Only then do people take ownership and responsibility for their work. It happens bottom up. We did not make an outside function responsible for quality and have them impose rules. We took the managers and people responsible for doing the work and let it be theirs. At first people said it would *never* happen. 'We'll never be allowed to follow a realistic process.' If you mentioned the old red SDM [Standard Development Methodology] book, people would laugh at you. They'd say, '*We just do what we're told.*'

We made our people a promise. If our people established a process and followed it, those processes would be respected. That promise was a shield. It put the people in a position of power. They are able to do their work based on their professional judgment. (See Figure 14.1.)

Now we're facing reality. Part of our process is putting realistic estimates on projects. Our people have been doing this work for years, they know what it takes. Management is supposed to say: 'we trust you.' They slip back into old habits sometimes, too. I know it comes from pressure they're feeling from *their* managers. But, when it happens, it's disappointing."

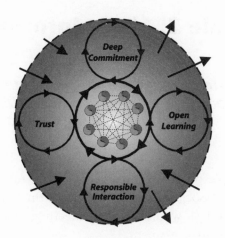

FIGURE 14.1
Keys to Synergy, Social, Human, and Intellectual Capital.

He stopped to think. "Can you imagine the power we'd have if everyone learned to work this way?"

> ### *You can't be partners with someone you are afraid of.*
> —LEE ZIMSKIND, DIRECTOR OF RESOURCE PLANNING

"I think there are two big benefits from the documentation process. First, risk management. Risk management is a process we are always looking to improve. By making the risks visible to management—and there are always risks, of course—we can be prepared in case they do happen. Everyone needs to know as early as possible if there are problems that need to be fixed." Lee paused to emphasize this point: "*You can't be partners with someone you are afraid of.* If you are really partners with your boss, you shouldn't be hiding things. There should be no surprises.

"When I was managing a team, I used to say: 'You need to give me a chance to help you, not tell me there's a problem when it's too late.' And, by the way, your boss shouldn't be saying, 'Only bring solutions to my office, not problems.' This just drives people away."

Simple Rule 2: Share Information

By listening and learning in front of my
people, I try to set an example.
—VINCE PASSIONE, GROUP MANAGER
PRODUCT DESIGN AND DEVELOPMENT

"Here's an example of what it's all about. Chris, my coach from BDA [Business Design Associates[2] is a consulting firm that helps teams to remove vicious cycles], would sit in on meetings and occasionally ask permission to give an assessment."

Vince pauses to explain. "That's the jargon we learn in our training. A BDA assessment is someone's point-in-time perspective of what is going on at that time. Anyone can do it, any time, anywhere. You start by asking permission of the person who will receive the assessment. The assessment can be positive or negative."

"So one day Chris asked permission to make an assessment—right in the middle of a meeting, in front of 35 of my staff members! I said, 'OK.' "

" 'Vince, you become passionate.' Chris was direct. He continued, 'You become self-righteous and stop listening, create blindness in yourself.' "

"Then a staff member popped up, 'When you don't listen, we feel you don't trust anybody here!' The dialogue that followed was very useful to everyone. To be effective, we all have to listen to messages about ourselves and be willing to learn. By listening and learning in front of my people, I try to set an example: to let them know it's OK to have flaws and not know everything. A lot of managers here feel like they're expected to be omnipotent. You can't learn to coordinate better by sitting up there on high!"

There were some sessions that might, at best,
be called fiery! But even those helped
to shape something: We learned
to work together.
—DAVE HALPIN, FINANCIAL CONTROL UNIT MANAGER

"Nine or ten years ago down in the [bleeped-out location] we went the SDLC [Standard Development Life Cycle] route. A waterfall method was imposed on us from the top down and, as you can guess, it didn't work. It might have been OK for some classical COBOL shop at that time but, for us, trying to follow it was a disaster. We spent all our time figuring out work-arounds. It had no meaning. We hated it. We kept back-dated time-and-date stamps for material we created after the fact in time for reviews. Looking back now, it's a little humorous, embarrassing, and pathetic. All that paper we produced wasn't real or integral to the process. What a waste!

In contrast, the effort worked here because it was bottom up. We asked the people doing the work: 'What would you do?' " He grimaced. "There were some sessions that might, at best, be called fiery! But even those helped to shape something: We learned to work together. We learned about consensus. We've made our defined process equal our real one. Do you have any idea how powerful that is?"

Simple Rule 3: Align Choices

If we're ever going to make this place less painful to work in, we've got to persist.
—Darlene Shuman, Savings and Relationship Pricing Development Manager

"It's been an enormous struggle for us to put real project plans in place and follow them. This is completely different from the old industry-wide habit of plan and ignore. Some days I'd just want to give up or drop out. Then I'd ask myself, 'Who am I hurting?' The answer was me and my staff. Sometimes I'd get tired fighting, especially on days when there'd be mixed messages from above. Then I'd remind myself: 'If we're ever going to make this place less painful to work in, we've got to persist.' I believe this is the right way to go. My heart's in the right place. But habits are hard to break; the mind and body aren't there yet.

The hardest part is finding the right level of detail for planning and tracking. Too much detail and we get drowned in making changes as things evolve. Too little and we don't have enough information to learn from for the next time around.

There's always pressure to move faster. Right now it *does* take us a little longer to get things done. I really believe this won't be the case once we truly get our new behavior turned into habits. I have to keep reminding people that now we no longer need time and resources for fixing things up after the fact."

We build on sand if we don't work on how we commit to each other.
—MIKE MCGEE, DEVELOPMENT MANAGER
FOR TAX SHELTER PROGRAMS

"I also had to remember that I'm not alone; I'm not the whole team. I always jumped into action, wasting the time of people I worked with. I was making bad requests to my team. Considering they didn't understand my requests, they did the best they could. In retrospect, I know there was no way they could have understood my requests. *I* didn't understand them. I hadn't given them enough thought. A BDA consultant told me that I could do this better if I wanted to. I took the challenge personally. Finally, the commitment thing crystalized in my mind. We build on sand if we don't work on how we commit to each other.

Some older, more senior managers fool themselves. They believe they have nothing to learn. They say the words about making level 3 and bringing strict discipline into the organization, but they don't have any themselves. They don't understand themselves. I see them in meetings with meaningless data, charts, dates, and agendas. It all *looks* like a process. But there's no commitment to their process, and they just don't see it. Many people at the senior level in a hierarchy can't see what's happening anymore; they forget what it's all about.

What it gets down to is actually caring about people you work with. Not inconveniencing them! Simply helping them to be the best they can be."

Simple Rule 4: Coordinate Co-evolution

*I was going full bore and was in the middle
of saying: "this is what we're going to do . . ."
when Jim stood up and said "no."*
—Cecil Wade, Corporate Financial Systems
Application Development Manager

"One day the head of quality assurance was out sick. We had a crisis and needed to fix a production bug. I called in Jim, the second in command, and began laying out the game plan. I was going full bore and was in the middle of saying: 'This is what we're going to do . . .' when Jim stood up and said '*no.*'

It bowled me over. And I said to myself, 'I have to think about this.' Of course, Jim was right. He knew it and stood up for it. It was a moment of revelation. There's a lot of project due-date worship and bowing to authority around here . . . and everywhere in business. Often they're false gods; we need to stand up and say *no.*"

*Last year when audit came in, we blew
them away.*
—Paul Doelger, Corporate Financial Systems
Software Quality Assurance

Paul tells the story of how surprised the Citibank auditors were, after only a year, to see the effects of the new habits of true participation and documenting the actual process. "Last year when audit came in, we blew them away with the changes in our group. They found *every single person—without exception*—knew what was in the plan and was actually doing it. The auditors rapidly saw the value of what we were doing. Like all of us, the CMM [the SEI Software Capability Maturity Model—an evolutionary fitness model for software development] was a difficult concept for the auditors as first. Now they've seen that it works here."

He smiled. "They're even comfortable calling me with questions when they're doing audits in other shops working with the CMM."

To conclude this chapter, we asked two of the leaders to speak directly to others considering whether they should apply an evolutionary fitness model in their businesses.

From One Leader to Others: What Does It Take to Engage an Evolutionary Fitness Model?

"What would I tell anybody else trying to do this?" Mike McGee considered and presented this list:

- *"First, it takes a big commitment from the manager. You have to be ready to do things you're not comfortable doing. That's a risk. Trusting others was the hardest for me."*

- *"Second, it takes time."*

- *"Third, give the model to the people. Bring your staff with you from the beginning."*

- *"Fourth, the model builds bottom-up, but managers have to reinforce things top-down. After it gets going, things take off by themselves. You begin to feel like you can change the world; you're empowered. Then, when you get the wrong message from management, the door slams, momentum stops, and you've got to generate it again. I can't say this enough:* It really takes commitment."

- *"My fifth suggestion is to work with BDA on the request and commitment stuff. I'll tell you why. Part of our hurdle was getting over my reputation as a hard nose. People were afraid of me. I keep thinking about the example of habits. 'Did you brush your teeth? Did you brush your teeth?' Consistent messages."*

"My messages were mixed. People saw me as a pusher, getting stuff done. Inside I was trying to get people out of here by 5:00 p.m. I'm married and have five kids. My family's important. I want people to work and get out of here. BDA helped me see how my sense of urgency came across."

From One Leader to Others: Why Should You Do This?

"I'll admit it now, I felt dragged into it. Not that we didn't need to improve," Dave Halpin shrugged. "But it's paid for itself over and over a thousand times." He ticked off the evidence of success on his fingers:

- *"First, we all feel more in control of our lives."*
- *"Second, we see patterns that make things more predictable."*
- *"Third, we're getting more work done."*
- *"Fourth, trust is up and our turnover rate is down."*
- *"Fifth, people understand the priorities."*
- *"Sixth, people like to come to work.*

"Anybody considering an effort such as this should know that *it's not easy but it does work."* Dave continued. "The right chemistry is really important: insiders and outsiders, managers and workers, communication and tenacity. The model just needs time to catch on and evolve."

Chapter Fifteen

The Citi Never Sleeps:
Persistence and Paradox

U sing interdisciplinary concepts, methods, and models of self-organizing systems, we see the overall enterprise emerging from the nonlinear interactions of its parts (people that work there). Any business can be reviewed considering the following key complexity concepts, which are rich in definition and important to business success:

- *Punctuated equilibrium*
- *Bounded instability*
- *Autopoiesis*
- *Co-evolution*
- *Sustainability*

Looking at an enterprise through these lenses helps us to observe and solve its current practical problems as well as foresee its possibilities for tomorrow. Through complexity science, we develop an *eye for paradox*, seeking the places where order and chaos coexist in a state of simultaneous transformation and stability and where unity and diversity give rise to one another. The *persistent* enterprise thrives in this breeding ground—a field of healthy tension created by coexisting extremes. It is paradox—not balance—that reveals the opportunities for successful co-evolution and potential for long-term existence despite a changing landscape.

The Citi in a Changing Landscape

In the fall of 1996, Brian Arthur, the Citibank Professor at the Santa Fe Institute, published an article entitled "Increasing Returns and the New World of Business" in *The Harvard Business Review*.[1] In the article, he discussed the changing nature of competitive business advantages in western economies:

- *From relying on bulk-material manufacturing to the design and use of technology*
- *From processing of resources to processing of information*
- *From delivering commodity products to delivering knowledge-based products*
- *From the application of raw energy to the application of ideas*
- *From repetitive day-to-day operations to the quest for innovation*
- *From emphasizing quality, low-cost production to a goal of being first (not always best) in the market with attendant high-cost research and development*
- *From branding and emergent-price standards to market lock-ins and high margins*
- *From a model of diminishing returns to a model of increasing returns*

Ironically, Citibank, along with the rest of the financial services industry, has for some time been struggling with both sets of characteristics. Citi's operations can be viewed as repetitive bulk processing. Yet, almost without warning, industry players can be disintermediated by phenomena associated with technology breakthrough and increasing returns.

Using Complexity Science to Explain Experience at Citibank

The following section presents a view of our experience at Citibank through the lenses of complexity. A great deal has been written about Citibank, and we do not intend to repeat a comprehensive description at this time. Rather, we present a selection of events and descriptions that we invite you to examine using the ideas from our model. This is an opportunity—a thought experiment—to try out the power of this framework.

Point 1: Working Punctuated Equilibrium

A study of complexity and fitness landscapes suggests that there should be a tension between the ability to climb higher on those fitness peaks where the business is already located and the capacity to leap to new peaks. A successful business recognizes this paradox and is able to do both. In addition, powerful businesses must have the capacity to respond effectively to avalanches and, in the best of all worlds, be able to trigger avalanches of their own (for example, generating a completely new market based on a unique use of a newly developing technology).

Does this happen in practice? There have been times when Citi has climbed out from under the avalanche of unexpected change; on the other hand, the bank has also successfully triggered a number of their own positive avalanches to change in the industry.

Outsiders have long considered Citicorp, based in New York City but with tentacles all over the United States and the world, as banking's trend setter. It has paved the way for virtually every advance in modern banking, from creating negotiable certificates of deposit (in 1961), to being the first bank to launch automated teller machines on a large scale in the late 1970's, to establishing an elaborate satellite network for electronic banking and moving ahead with interstate banking in the early 80's. One of its innovations, the bank holding company, propelled it outside of banking. Citicorp is the bank holding company of which Citibank is the largest unit.[2]

By 1984, Citicorp, parent company of Citibank, was the largest bank in the world, having overtaken rivals one by one, such as Chase Manhattan and Chemical. Citibank was widely perceived as one of the most, if not the most, competitive, innovative, and successful banking companies.

This was the legacy that John S. Reed inherited as Chairman Walter Wriston retired and passed the baton in his direction. John had made his mark in the seventies by using computerized systems to clean up the tangle of paper that was Citi's back-office operation. Internally, he was famous for his *Memo from the Beach* (written while on vacation) in which he made clear his vision of distributed decision-making and autonomy in the context of a multinational corporation.

Strangely enough, "People are not vying against each other within a predetermined hierarchy at Citicorp. 'It's very decentralized here,' explained a young manager in the data processing department. 'There are lots of small organizations at Citibank, so you feel you can rise to the top of something.'[3] 'I came here because I knew that if I busted my fanny and worked hard I would be able to get ahead,' explained a young auditor from New York City."[4]

Bottom Line for Point 1: Punctuated Equilibrium

At Citibank, leaders and agents:

- *Make incremental evolutionary progress (climbing industry fitness peaks)* and *make bold moves to leap to new fitness peaks (leaving an avalanche of industry "catch-up" in our wake)*

- *Have a clear vision and corporate strategic direction (owning fitness peaks)* yet *leave some room for local innovation and experimentation (looking for desirable new peaks)*

- *Maintain focus on the discipline of daily execution and performance (owning space on the landscape)* and *are able to be vision-*

ary, futuristic, and risk-taking (triggering avalanches and creating new landscapes)

Point 2: Maintaining Bounded Instability

If increasingly complex and successful entities emerge from points of bounded instability, then we should expect Citibank to have both boundaries and a history of crossing those boundaries.

By the mid-80s, Citicorp had emerged as an organization that was bound and determined to bring avalanches of change to banking. Its people had created an internal network and infrastructure to maintain this bounded instability. Amplifying feedback loops accelerated learning and action based on successful risk-taking. With management of course providing leadership, the Citicorp entrepreneurial system was self-generating. Everyone at Citibank talked of the externally focused competitive atmosphere, which had internally emerged from the people and their patterns of interaction. Using expressions such as war rooms (conference rooms were literally labeled this way), bunker down, scout out the enemy, bite the bullet, and hold the fort, Citibank's language—Citispeak—reflected the enterprise view of a well-organized global campaign for market dominance.

Sometimes the entrepreneurial amplification was characterized as reaching a runaway state with the bank itself being accused of taking shortcuts. Although, for example, a 1983 *Fortune* article detailed the case of dubious international currency-trading practices, others would later conclude that, "For the most part, however, Citibank's brash moves have paid off, especially on the bottom line."[5]

Bottom Line for Point 2: Bounded Instability

We notice that Citibank straddles further paradox:

- *Both recognition and development of core competency (clear boundaries) and boldness in making moves that cross those boundaries (shaking things up and working far from equilibrium)*
- *Development of units and managers optimizing the core (stability) and development of units and managers that introduce innovation and new business (instability)*

Point 3: Developing Conscious Autopoiesis

In the course of our work, we have examined the age-old question, "What is life?" "How does it work?" "How can a living organism learn, mature, and change—and still be the same entity?" If it is possible to apply the concept of autopoiesis to businesses, we should expect that studies of Citibank would show evidence of both strong organizational memes as well as considerable emergent self-organization—another paradox. Sure enough, we've verified that such evidence exists.

The Citibank "personality" is well documented, and Citibankers are known around the world for doing things the Citi way—with a determinedly individual interpretation. In the mid-1980s, Citicorp was included in *The 100 Best Companies to Work for in America* and was ranked among the top 10 in employee opportunity for advancement.[6] The entrepreneurial memes and culture had become extremely powerful. Over time, this culture had learned to propagate itself. "Citicorp attracts a distinct breed: people who relish action. People who thrive on competition. People who love pressure."[7] People who enjoy being fully autonomous agents. Stuffy banker types or folks averse to hard work didn't enter the fold. Those who did were quickly identified by the "immune" system as not fitting and ejected like a virus.

Bottom Line for Point 3: Conscious Autopoeisis

Citibank's persistence has been attributed to:

- *Cultural consistency (self-similarity across the organization)* and *operational autonomy (self-organization through autonomous agents)*

- *A relatively fixed underlying belief system (fractal organization) yet resilience and readiness for change and variation (room for emerging patterns of behavior)*

- *Extremely tight culture (almost cultlike: "the way we do things at Citibank" applied at all nested levels) but a pride of local authorship and a tendency to twist and tweak (local adaptation and experimentation with change)*

Point 4: Co-evolving at Micro- and Macrolevels

According to theories of cognitive evolution, organisms maintain themselves, mature, and adjust to their environments. We would expect a long-lived, persistent enterprise to do the same and to do it at a variety of nested levels from the micro to the macro. As evidenced in the following, Citibankers make internal incremental evolutionary progress, *at the same time* constantly adapting with the bank's changing economic, market, and regulatory environments.

John Reed became interested in complexity, as a way to gain insight into a turbulent economic environment. "Under Reed's predecessor, Citicorp had just taken a bath in the Third World debt crisis. The bank had lost $1 billion in profits in one year and was still sitting on $13 billion of loans that might never be paid back."[8]

Although Citicorp's year-end share price in 1989 was at a 20-year high of $28.88, the economic fitness landscapes were again changing. By year-end 1990, share price had plummeted to $12.63—a near 20-year low (that would bottom out at $8.50 before it was all over). The bank was temporarily below the Bank for International Settlements' minimums for capitalization. The Federal Reserve dropped a Memo of Understanding on Citi.

Faced with multiple avalanches, "Reed concluded that the best management philosophy for the bank was to constrain growth within the limits of each market and to excel at the control aspects of the business: expenses and credit quality," wrote *Euromoney Magazine*. "Citicorp had to do the *opposite of what it had been doing for the previous twenty years*. This was the genesis of a Five-Point Plan to improve the bank's operating earnings sufficiently to absorb the coming credit costs."[9]

The plan was nothing if not ambitious. It required that Citicorp focus on the short-term in 1991 and 1992, cut costs by $1.5 billion a year, trim the senior management, raise $4 to $5 billion in capital, and do so without selling off or hurting the core consumer and commercial business franchises around the world. A complete antithesis to their well-established patterns of interaction, this was a tall order for a highly decentralized organization staffed with trend-setting autonomous agents.

And so it was that Citibank entered survival mode and fought to endure waves of culture shock as cost-and-credit management became a corporate obsession and was applied in a top-down command-and-control manner. Management pushed. Staff pushed back. Management pushed again. Implementation of the plan reflected the life-and-death struggle of the macrosystem with its microparts.

Citibank reduced its workforce from 96,000 to 81,000. Management changes at even the highest levels were thick and fast. The parts were coupled in patterns that did not meet the needs of the new environment. Triggered by this rapidly forced change, the whole system and its nested subsystems self-organized for survival. In some corners of the bank, vicious cycles began to emerge. The Five-Point Plan met its goals, but the success of the plan came at substantial cost.

In January 1993, Citibank was able to trumpet success when it released its 1992 year-end earnings. Justifiably proud of his work, John Reed sent out a news release in which he said: "The plan's goals have been achieved. Citicorp's priorities for 1993 are to focus on balance sheet and earnings performance, on executional competence and cost discipline, on our business franchises, our customers and our people."

Bottom Line for Point 4: Co-evolution

As Citibank pulled through and those that survived breathed a sign of relief, they fantasized about getting back to normal—back to the way things used to be. But history is important in self-organizing systems; and, they can't go backward—they're irreversible. Instead, Citi continued to co-evolve.

Point 5: Sustaining the Business and Its Ecosystem

From the study of ecology, we would expect that to survive for longer than a decade, a business would need not only to aggressively pursue its own survival, both short and long term, but also to attend to the industry, markets, and communities in which it is situated. Without an ecosystem in which to function, a business should not be able to survive. It will be no surprise that this brings us to the final points of apparently paradoxical behavior at Citibank.

We recognize that we are now living in a world far different from the one in which Citibank experienced its initial spurt of growth. Throughout the 1990s we have felt the effects of living in a continually evolving corporation within a complex and changing market environment. We see that the impact of today's global economy on our customers and, in turn, on us is profound. We have felt the push to develop Citibank's level of fitness to avoid a repeat of our 1990 experience.

Who would have thought, 10 years ago, that IBM and General Motors—the largest industrial companies of the world, companies with tens of billions of dollars in revenue a month—would go through massive restructuring? Who would have thought that many of our Fortune 500 customers would no longer be on the list? Who would have predicted the extent to which we and our customers would be bound to the Asian and Russian economies—that something called the Internet would today be a source of major business opportunity for all of us?

As a corporation, Citibank has gone through a lot of change but our evolution continues. To Citi's management, fitness means a focus on day-to-day performance and an ability to execute internally without major disruptions or disasters from external change. As part of enhancing Citibank's capability, management wants to avoid being surprised by avalanches of change—unexpected external happen-stance that forces an internal ad hoc reaction to it.

We cannot limit tomorrow's change or eliminate today's problems, but we must accept that both will happen. The big issue is how we will respond under the circumstances. One of Citi's senior managers has gone as far as to suggest that any difficulties Citi has had in the recent past have had more to do with reaction to events rather than the events in and of themselves. And his answer to the dilemma is to be in contact with reality and see things for what they are. This means spotting problems or opportunities as they emerge and responding to them in a timely and thoughtful manner; being seen by customers as paying attention and caring; and keeping innovation, quality, and responsiveness alive and well.

Although Reed didn't have the benefit of a formal evolutionary fitness model to follow, he was, in effect, describing a need to enable more effective co-evolution:

- *Internally—developing the ability to respond (which takes place as an organization moves to levels 2 and 3 in the complexity advantage evolutionary fitness model)*

- *Externally—developing the ability to create more reliable scenarios amid changing fitness landscapes (which takes place as a business moves to level 4 in the complexity advantage evolutionary fitness model)*

Bottom Line for Point 5: Sustainability

Citibank has:

- *Practical respect for the shareholder (the health of the individual business) and for other stakeholders as well (health of the eco-system)*

- *Demands for bottom-line performance (immediate survival) and investment in the future (survival over the long term)*

Citibank Today

As we are completing this chapter, Citibank is maintaining its leadership role. The January 24, 1998, issue of *The Economist* begins an article about a possible new Citibank strategy with the declaration: "In international consumer banking, there is only one success story: Citibank. While dozens of institutions have tried to cross borders, Citi stands alone in making itself the bank of choice for wealthy businessmen around the world."[10]

And then, on April 6, the following press release announced even more Citi evolution and triggered unprecedented avalanches of merger mania throughout the U.S. financial services industry.

CITICORP AND TRAVELERS GROUP TO MERGE, CREATING
CITIGROUP: THE GLOBAL LEADER IN FINANCIAL SERVICES
Combined Company Will Be Poised to Deliver
a Full Range of Products and Services
to Over 100 Million Customers in 100 Countries

Transaction Has a Value of Over $140 Billion

New York, NY, April 6, 1998—Citicorp (NYSE:CCI) and
Travelers Group (NYSE:TRV) today announced an agreement to merge, forming the global leader in financial services. The combination will bring together two
organizations with core commitments to serving consumers, corporations, institutions and governments
globally, through a diverse array of sales and service
channels. The merged company's principal thrusts will
be traditional banking, consumer finance, credit cards,
investment banking, securities brokerage and asset management, and property casualty and life insurance.

The combined company, which will be named Citigroup
Inc. and use the trademark Travelers red umbrella as its
logo, will serve over 100 million customers in 100 countries around the world. On a proforma basis, the company
would have had assets at year-end 1997 of almost $700 bil-
lion, net revenues of nearly $50 billion, operating income
of approximately $7.5 billion and equity of more than $44
billion. Its market capitalization would rank it number
one among the world's financial services companies.

Mr. Reed and Mr. Weill said in a statement: "Citicorp and
Travelers Group bring together some of the best people
in the financial services business, creating a resource for
customers like no other—a diversified global consumer
financial services company, a premier global bank, a
leading global asset management company, a preemi-
nent global investment banking and trading firm, and a
broad-based insurance capability. Our ability to serve

consumers, corporations, institutions, and government agencies, domestic and foreign, will be without parallel. This is a combination whose time has come."

Today, not all of Citi is yet riding a hypercycle. A new culture has not had time to evolve. Citibankers are engaged in quality initiatives and focused on cultural change aimed at imbedding new habits throughout the new company. Constant vigilance is needed from everyone in the enterprise to 1) continually create new, innovative, and reliable customer products and services and 2) habitually deliver "better, faster, and cheaper" on an ongoing basis. This diligence is not yet tightly woven into the fiber of Citigroup. It is something that, with focused attention, can evolve to sustain Citigroup as one of the New Breed in the financial services industry.

Improving internal capabilities is slow and difficult but possible. By engaging the Software CMM model, Citibank started the process of developing local teams that have the ability to understand their true capabilities, make their processes visible, and engage in true dialogue about them, and—therefore—to be able to make deep commitments *and to change rapidly when needed:* not only to stop but to turn on a dime. Citi is well positioned to build on its history of autonomy and engage the complexity advantage evolutionary fitness model more broadly throughout the organization. By enlisting additional evolutionary models in functional areas outside of software development, the bank can reap the full rewards of Reed's investment in complexity science.

The Next 4 Billion Years

We invite you to now test *your* business against the concepts and steps we've presented here. We suggest you conduct this test by trying out a story about businesses that thrive in the midst of complexity. Again, using the five key concepts (punctuated equilibrium, bounded instability, autopoiesis, co-evolution, and sustainability), decide whether such a story feels right to you in light of your own practical experience.

Here Is the Story

Businesses that maintain a paradoxical existence in a complex environment use strategies to fit with that environment and at the same time to position themselves to cause, or adapt in the event of, industry avalanches or changes to that environment (punctuated equilibrium). Such businesses have the flexibility to adjust to changing environments by maintaining "stable" core competencies that transition from time to time due to "fringe" efforts nearly at a point of chaos (bounded instability). Thriving businesses use self-organization to regulate yet continually renew themselves at a rate in keeping with industry power laws. They are structured as a web of diverse autonomous agents yet are unified through self-similarity in core values, permeable team boundaries, and earned power. These businesses become self-bounded, self-generated, and self-perpetuating (consciously autopoietic). The parts maintain the success of the whole, and the whole perpetuates the success of the parts. Autopoietic organizations persist by leveraging human, social, and intellectual capital to adjust their internal relationships and external partnerships for increased fitness (co-evolution). These powerful elements—cycling in closed loops with open feedback—enable fitness to emerge even in changing landscapes (sustainability).

Living the Story

In the spirit of Peppermint Patty—the girl with the errant hair in Charles Schulz's *Peanuts* cartoon strip who engages true-and-false tests with enthusiasm and the utter certainty of the very young, declaiming: "TRUE, FALSE, TRUE, ABSOLUTELY TRUE"—we have just given you a generative test of our recommendations. We do not expect—or even want—utter certainty on the part of our readers, but hope, instead, it will provide a starting point or baseline for your own "fitness program."

Remember, it's a three-part program:

Part 1: Engage the Four Simple Rules to Remove Vicious Cycles and Install Hypercycles

1. Generate and exchange collaborative energy.

2. Share the history of important perturbations and the insights gleaned.

3. Only make commitments that you truly believe you will be able to meet.

4. Embrace constant change in a disciplined but resilient manner to co-evolve.

Part 2: Use the 14 Steps to Ascend the Complexity Advantage Evolutionary Fitness Model

Fitness Level 1: Unconscious Self-Organization

At level 1, start by fully investigating and recognizing the state of the business. The unconscious focus at level 1 is on agent self-preservation. Determine the extent of existing dysfunctional cycles—likely to be masked by surface compliance to command-and-control environments—and remove them. A professionally guided self-assessment is key to a clear understanding of the situation. Then use steps 1 through 8 to move to level 2.

1. Adopt the new sciences.

2. Create urgency of purpose for sustaining the global enterprise.

3. Develop a web of diverse agents and visionary leaders.

4. Count on closed loops to achieve unity.

5. Drive out fear and grow trust.

6. Build commitment across stakeholder boundaries.

7. Improve constantly and forever every process supporting co-evolution.

8. Institute open learning for everyone.

Fitness Level 2: Conscious Self-Organization

At level 2, businesses have many committed and disciplined local teams that recognize their self-organization and use it to leverage accurate information and accumulated knowledge. Because their processes are visible, these teams have developed the means to understand and adjust their capabilities. The focus is at the team level, and developing functional patterns of interaction among teams is the next step. To move to level 3, where effective patterns of micro- and macrocoupling emerge, businesses use complexity advantage steps 9 and 10, developing synergy and social capital.

9. Do business on the basis of synergy and collaboration to maximize customer satisfaction.

10. Generate social capital by offering employability and new possibilities to the workforce.

Fitness Level 3: Guided Self-Organization

At level 3, linked teams enable the business to propagate successful lessons learned and functional interlocking patterns of behavior across larger units within the business. To reach level 4 and secure the benefits of quantitative and complexity-based models throughout the organization, businesses focus on step 11. In addition, leaders use step 12 to engage all autonomous agents within the business to increase human capital resources and the use of common sense.

11. Adopt statistical thinking, nonlinear mathematics, and complexity models for insight.

12. Encourage people to take pride in product and service delivery and the enterprise to benefit from human capital.

Fitness Level 4: Quantitatively Guided Self-Organization

At level 4, the business functions smoothly as a whole enterprise composed of autonomous agents, reorganizing themselves as necessary and using quantitative tools effectively. To move to level 5 and have the ability to sustain itself in the face of avalanches and rapidly changing landscapes, the business must attend not only to internal people, processes, and patterns, but also to those on the outside—especially those closely coupled with the business's interests. Steps 13 and 14 provide guidance to those making this move.

13. Seed innovation and harvest intellectual capital from everyone.

14. Sustain and enjoy conscious, competent, co-evolution.

Fitness Level 5: Consciously Competent Autopoiesis

To get the feeling of potential power at level 5, we want to replay several statements from earlier chapters. Remember when Silvana Lipovac said: "Besides, here you're able to do what's right for yourself and for your organization. I've been shocked at just how good it feels to have this autonomy, ability, and . . . *power!*" (And this was just at level 2.)

While celebrations are certainly in order when reaching level 5, sustaining a competitive edge requires constant vigilance. Silvana knew this too: "And we're not done. *There is no such thing as done.* There's only constant learning. There's so much to keep up on. I never stop reading now."

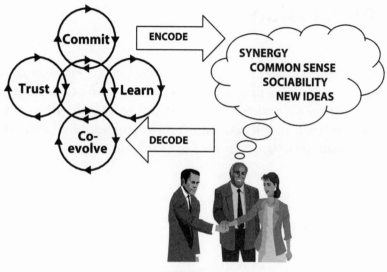

FIGURE 15.1
Conscious Co-evolution.

Fully engaged autonomy requires discipline and hard work but generates the ability to sustain successful co-evolution (see Figure 15.1). Sidney Gottesman put it well: "Can you imagine the power we'd have if everyone learned to work this way?"

Part 3: Use Your Complexity Skills to Trigger External Selection

We have focused on the levels of internal self-organization without attending to the selection that takes place in the external environment based on the level of enterprise fitness. We have done this because we believe that internal fitness is the first, but—it is very important to say—not the only sequence in effective co-evolution. Complexity science can be used to monitor and predict possible ranges of actions for other entities—as well as to suggest the changing nature of the economic landscape and the likelihood of avalanches of change.

In Conclusion

Please feel free to build on what we've offered here. Our theories have been built on the work of others. If they help you in achieving greater fitness in whatever business landscape you've chosen, we will have achieved our goal. It will take all of us working as fully autonomous agents to continue to thrive in the next 4 billion years.

Notes

Chapter Two
Key Complexity Advantage Concepts
1. Letter, 19 December 1935, published in *Letters of Wallace Stevens 336,* Holly Stevens (ed.) (New York: Alfred A. Knopf, 1967).

Chapter Four
Old and New Models
1. On January 30, 1998, http://www.santafe.edu/
2. M. Mitchell Waldrop, *Complexity: The Emerging Science at the Edge of Order and Chaos* (New York: Simon and Schuster [Touchstone], 1992, pp. 91, 96).
3. Business Design Associates, 1420 Harbor Bay Parkway, Suite 200, Alameda, CA 94502. 510-814-1900. info@bda.com
4. KLG Productivity Associates, Inc., 60 East 42nd Street, New York, NY 10165. 212-286-9652. www.mindspring.com/~tl-klg
5. Statisticians collect and classify data in numerical characteristics and then use these data to make inferences and predictions. Generally, they take measurements from a small group (the sample) and use them to predict the behavior of a larger group (the population). The probability theory is used to determine how well the sample represents the population (known as *the degree of confidence*).

Chapter Five
Surviving in Fear
1. George Santayana, *Reason in Common Sense: The Life of Reason, Vol. 1* (New York: C. Scribner's Sons, 1905–1906).
2. Dilbert website. On November 27, 1997. http://www.unitedmedia.com/comics/dilbert

Chapter Six
Thriving on Trust
1. Herodotus, *The Histories of Herodotus,* Book I, Chapter 8, Walter Blanco (trans.) (New York: Norton, 1992).
2. Human Synergistics, 39819 Plymouth Road, Plymouth, MI 48170. 313-459-1030.
3. Walter A Shewhart, *Statistical Method from the Viewpoint of Quality Control,* W. Edwards Deming (ed.) (Washington, D.C.: The Graduate School, The Department of Agriculture, 1939).

Chapter Seven
Fourteen Steps for Success

1. Tom Polen, "Statistical Thinking—A Personal Application," *Special Publication of the ASQ Statistics Division,* Spring 1996, pp. 18–23.
2. Philip Howard, *The Death of Common Sense: How Law Is Suffocating America* (New York: Warner Books, 1996).
3. W. Edwards Deming, *Out of the one Crisis* (Cambridge, MA: MIT Center for Advanced Engineering Study, 1982, pp. 23–24).

Chapter Eight
Introducing Evolutionary Fitness Models

1. Carnegie Mellon University Software Engineering Institute, *The Capability Maturity Model: Guidelines for Improving the Software Process* (Reading, MA: Addison-Wesley Publishing, 1995, Foreword).
2. P. Crosby, *Eternally Successful Organization: The Art of Corporate Wellness* (New York: McGraw-Hill, 1992).

Chapter Nine
The Complexity Advantage Evolutionary Fitness Model

1. Dilbert website. On November 27, 1997. http://www.unitedmedia.com/comics/dilbert.

Chapter Ten
Autonomous Agents

1. Alfred Steinberg, *The Man from Missouri,* 1962. (As quoted in Bartlett, John, *Bartlett's Familiar Quotations, 16th Edition,* Justin Kaplan [general editor] [Boston: Little, Brown & Company, 1992, p. 655].)
2. Nikos Kazantzakis, *Zorba the Greek,* 1946. (As quoted in Bartlett, John, *Bartlett's Familiar Quotations, 16th Edition,* Justin Kaplan [general editor] [Boston: Little, Brown & Company, 1992, p. 652].)
3. As quoted in Anne Wilson Schaef, *365 Meditations for People Who (May) Worry Too Much* (New York: Workman, 7 January 1998).
4. John F. Kennedy, Inaugural Address, 10 January 1961. (As quoted in Bartlett, John, *Bartlett's Familiar Quotations, 16th Edition,* Justin Kaplan [general editor]. [Boston: Little, Brown & Company, 1992, p. 741].)

Chapter Eleven
Leaders

1. Jonathon Brent, *Battle Ground Berlin: CIA versus KGB in the Cold War* (New Haven, CT: Yale University Press, 1997, p. xxv).
2. *The Columbia Dictionary of Quotations* is licensed from Columbia University Press. Copyright © 1993 by Columbia University Press. All rights reserved. (Quoted in Tamara Deutsche, *Not By Politics Alone,* ch. 2, 1973, to Kropotkin in May 1919.)
3. Edward Yourdon, *Decline and Fall of the American Programmer* (Englewood Cliffs, NJ: Yourdon Press, 1992).

Chapter Twelve
Catalysts
1. Thomas Alva Edison, *Life,* 1932.

Chapter Thirteen
Eco-Technicians
1. Andrew P. Sage, "Toward Systems Ecology," *Computer: Innovative technology for computer professionals,* February 1998, p. 110. © 1998 IEEE.
2. Andrew P. Sage, "Toward Systems Ecology," *Computer: Innovative technology for computer professionals,* February 1998, pp. 107–110. © 1998 IEEE.
3. Marshall McLuhan, *Understanding Media: The Extensions of Man, 2nd Edition* (New York: McGraw-Hill [Mentor Books], 1964, p. xi).
4. Andrew P. Sage, "Toward Systems Ecology," *Computer: Innovative technology for computer professionals,* February 1998, p. 110. © 1998 IEEE.
5. Andrew P. Sage, "Toward Systems Ecology," *Computer: Innovative technology for computer professionals,* February 1998, pp. 107–110. © 1998 IEEE.
6. CASA, 1911 Central Avenue, Los Alamos, NM 87544. 505-662-6820. jrd@lacasa.com

Chapter Fourteen
Experiencing the Advantage
1. William Shakespeare, *Macbeth,* V, v. 17 (London: Cornmarket, 1969).
2. Business Design Associates, 1420 Harbor Bay Parkway, Suite 200, Alameda, CA 94502. 510-814-1900. info@bda.com

Chapter Fifteen
The Citi Never Sleeps: Persistence and Paradox
1. W. Brian Arthur, "Increasing Returns and the New World of Business," *Harvard Business Review,* July-August 1996, pp. 100–109.
2. Robert Levering, Milton Moskowitz, and Michael Katz, *The 100 Best Companies to Work for in America* (New York: Addison-Wesley, 1984, p. 43).
3. Ibid., pp. 44–45.
4. Ibid., p. 45.
5. Roy Rowan, "The Maverick Who Yelled Foul at Citibank," *Fortune Magazine,* 107, no. 1 (January 20, 1983): 44–56.
6. Robert Levering, Milton Moskowitz, and Michael Katz, *The 100 Best Companies to Work for in America* (New York: Addison-Wesley, 1984, p. 43).
7. Ibid., p. 43.
8. M. Mitchell Waldrop, *Complexity: The Emerging Science at the Edge of Order and Chaos* (New York: Simon & Schuster, 1992, p. 91).
9. Peter Lee, "Citi Back from the Dead?" *Euromoney Magazine,* December 1992.
10. "Citibank, Trading Down," *The Economist,* 24 January 1998, pp. 73–74.

Bibliography

Argyris, Chris. *Knowledge for Action.* San Francisco: Jossey-Bass, 1993.

Bak, Per. *How Nature Works.* New York: Springer-Verlag, 1996.

Bateson, Gregory. *Steps to an Ecology of the Mind.* New York: Ballantine Books, 1972.

Bartlett, John. *Bartlett's Familiar Quotations, 16th Edition,* Justin Kaplan (general editor). Boston: Little, Brown & Company, 1992.

Bar-Yam, Yaneer. *Dynamics of Complex Systems: Studies in Nonlinearity.* New York: Addison-Wesley, 1997.

Burke, James, and Robert Ornstein. *The Axemaker's Gift: A Double-Edged History of Human Culture.* New York: Grosset/Putnam, 1995.

Capra, Fritjof. *The Web of Life: A New Scientific Understanding of Living Systems.* New York: Doubleday, 1996.

Collins, James C., and Jerry I. Porras. *Built to Last: Successful Habits of Visionary Companies.* New York: Harper Business, 1997.

Conner, Daryl R. *Managing at the Speed of Change.* New York: Random House, 1992.

Constantine, Larry L. *On Peopleware.* Englewood Cliffs, NJ: Yourdon Press, 1995.

Darwin, Charles. *The Origin of Species.* New York: Prometheus Books, 1991.

Dawkins, Richard. *The Selfish Gene.* Oxford: Oxford University Press, 1976.

Deming, W. Edwards. *Out of the Crisis.* Cambridge, MA: MIT Center for Advanced Engineering Study, 1982.

Dossey, Larry. *Space, Time & Medicine.* Boston: Shambhala, 1985.

Flores, Fernando, and Terry Winograd. *Understanding Computers and Cognition.* Norwood, NJ: Ablex Corp., 1986.

Fukuyama, Francis. *Trust: The Social Virtues and the Creation of Prosperity.* New York: Free Press, 1995.

Gamov, George. *Thirty Years That Shook Physics: The Story of Quantum Theory.* New York: Dover Publications, 1985.

Gleick, James. *Chaos: Making a New Science.* New York: Viking Penguin, 1987.

Goodwin, Brian. *How the Leopard Changed Its Spots: The Evolution of Complexity.* New York: Simon & Schuster (Touchstone Press), 1996.

Jencks, Charles. *The Architecture of the Jumping Universe: A Polemic: How Complexity Science Is Changing Architecture and Culture.* London: Academy Editions, 1995.

Kauffman, Stuart. *At Home in the Universe: The Search for the Laws of Self-Organization and Complexity.* New York: Oxford University Press, 1995.

Kelly, Kevin. *Out of Control: The New Biology of Machines, Social Systems and the Economic World.* New York: Addison Wesley, 1994.

Kelly, Kevin. "New Rules for the New Economy: Twelve Dependable Principles for Thriving in a Turbulent World." *Wired Magazine,* September 1997.

Kroeger, Otto, and Janet M. Thuesen. *Type Talk at Work: How the 16 Personality Types Determine Your Success on the Job.* New York: Dell, 1992.

Laszlo, Ervin. *The Systems View of the World*. New York: George Braziller, 1972.

Lee, Peter. "Citi Back from the Dead?" *Euromoney Magazine*, December 1992.

Mainzer, Klaus. *Thinking in Complexity*. Heidelberg: Springer-Verlag, 1994.

Maturana, Humberto R., and Francisco J. Varela. *The Tree of Knowledge: The Biological Roots of Human Understanding*, Rev. Ed. Boston: Shambhala, 1987.

"Maverick Who Yelled Foul at Citibank, The." *Fortune* Magazine, 1983.

Morrison, Ian. *The Second Curve: Managing the Velocity of Change*. New York: Random House, 1996.

Pascale, Richard Tanner. *Managing on the Edge*. New York: Simon & Schuster, 1990.

Prigogine, Ilya. *The End of Certainty: Time, Chaos, and the New Laws of Nature*. New York: Free Press, 1997.

Prigogine, Ilya, and Isabella Stengers. *Order out of Chaos: Man's New Dialogue with Nature*. New York: Bantam Books, 1984.

Senge, Peter M. *The Fifth Discipline: The Art & Practice of The Learning Organization*. New York: Doubleday Currency, 1990.

Shakespeare, William. *Macbeth*. London: Cornmarket, 1969.

Simon, Herbert A. *The Sciences of the Artificial, Third Edition*. Cambridge, MA: The MIT Press, 1996.

Software Engineering Institute, Carnegie Mellon University. *The Capability Maturity Model: Guidelines for Improving the Software Process*. Menlo Park, CA: Addison Wesley, 1995.

Van Der Ryn, Sim, and Stuart Cowan. *Ecological Design*. Washington, D.C.: Island Press, 1996.

Volk, Tyler. *Metapatterns: Across Space, Time and Mind*. New York: Columbia University Press, 1995.

Waldrop, M. Mitchell. *Complexity: The Emerging Science at the Edge of Chaos*. New York: Simon & Schuster, 1992.

Weiner, Norbert. *The Human Use of Human Beings: Cybernetics and Society*. New York: Plenum (Da Capo), 1954.

Wheatley, Margaret. *Leadership and the New Science*. San Francisco: Berrett-Koehler, 1992.

Zohar, Danah, and I. N. Marshall. *The Quantum Self: Human Nature and Consciousness Defined by the New Physics*. New York: William Morrow, 1990.

Index

ABOUT THE AUTHORS

Susanne Kelly is a vice president in Citibank's Corporate Technology Office, where she currently works as Research Director for Citibank's Complexity and Organizational Behavior Project. With over 20 years of high-powered business responsibility spanning the communications, technology, chemical manufacturing, and banking industries, she has had broad experience from marketing and customer service to technology development. Ms. Kelly is also a popular international speaker on Complexity and Organizational Behavior.

Mary Ann Allison is a principal in The Allison Group, LLC (www .allisongroup.com), a New York City consulting firm providing services, such as strategic planning, organizational development, and generating virtual communities, to companies ranging from start-ups to multinationals like Hewlett-Packard. Previously, she was a vice president at Citibank and president of an Internet start-up company. She is also the author of *Managing Up, Managing Down*, and speaks on complexity, business, and community.